Stumbling toward Utopia

*How the 1960s Turned into a
National Nightmare and How We Can
Revive the American Dream*

Tim Goeglein

FIDELIS
PUBLISHING

FIDELIS PUBLISHING®

ISBN: 9781956454475
ISBN (eBook): 9781956454482

Stumbling Toward Utopia
How the 1960s Turned into a National Nightmare and How We Can
Revive the American Dream

© 2024 Timothy S. Goeglein

Cover Design by Diana Lawrence
Interior Design by Xcel Graphic
Edited by Amanda Varian

Order at www.faithfultext.com for a significant discount. Email info@
fidelispublishing.com to inquire about bulk purchase discounts.

Fidelis Publishing, LLC • Winchester, VA / Nashville, TN •
fidelispublishing.com

Manufactured in the United States of America
10 9 8 7 6 5 4 3 2 1

FIDELIS
PUBLISHING

Contents

Introduction 1

Chapter One   Letters from a Pen Pal 13

Chapter Two   How the Stumbling Began 23

Chapter Three The Moral Stumble 49

Chapter Four   The Education Stumble 59

Chapter Five   The Entertainment Stumble 73

Chapter Six   The Fiscal Stumble 91

Chapter Seven The Family Stumble 103

Chapter Eight The Religious Stumble 129

Chapter Nine   The Civility Stumble 143

Chapter Ten   Reviving the Dream: The Road
               Back from the 1960s' Stumbles 153

Notes   161

Introduction

Between the 1960s and the 2000s, Americans went to war with one another.[1]
—Robert O. Self, Professor of History, Brown University

There's little doubt that the 1960s was a decade that changed the nation. What started out as an age of hopeful innocence grew into a time of rage and violence.[2]
—Melissa Erickson

To overcome the Sixties, we must first understand them. One must sometimes go back in time in order to move forward.[3]
—Judge J. Harvie Wilkinson III

According to Merriam-Webster's Dictionary, "in 1516, English humanist Sir Thomas More published a book titled *Utopia*, which compared social and economic conditions in Europe with those of an ideal society on an imaginary island located off the coast of the Americas. More wanted to imply that the perfect conditions on his fictional island could never really exist, so he called it 'Utopia,' a

1

name he created by combining the Greek words *ou* ('not, no') and *topos* ('place'). The current use of *utopia*, referring to an ideal place or society, was inspired by More's description of Utopia's perfection."[4] Utopia refers to an imaginary community or society that possesses highly desirable or near-perfect qualities for its members.

For centuries since More first coined the word, man has sought to create their own utopias where everything, in human understanding, would be perfect – a heaven on earth. Everyone would get along—there would be no poverty, no war, no conflict of any kind. It is a desire we all have because we are created Imago Dei—in the image of God—and thus yearn for such a place.

Unfortunately, all man's attempts to create a utopian society have been abject failures because they are based on man's efforts, instead of submission to God's authority. Only in heaven is such a utopia a reality. But that has not stopped them from trying. In 1971, John Lennon penned the utopian anthem, "Imagine," in which he called for a world without religion, without countries, with no possessions, no greed or hunger, and a brotherhood of man "sharing the world."[5]

Lennon's wistful thinking became the anthem for a more recent attempt to create another utopia. This attempt was fueled by the radical activists of the 1960s who unleashed the latest attempt to create a perfect, at least in their view, American society.

Instead, they took a wrecking ball to society and America has never been the same. All one has to do is look at our current culture to see the damage the 1960s utopians created.

Hardly a day goes by without someone asking me, "What happened to America?" or "How did we end up in such a mess?" For many, they feel they are living an American nightmare, rather than the American Dream.

America today is, sadly, a fractured country—fractured along religious, moral, and economic lines. As we look out at our country, we see young people—particularly young men—struggling to find purpose, settle down, and become productive members of society. Many are angry at their fate and lash out—as we have seen with the horrific shootings and other acts of violence over the past few years.

We also see young women who want to be married and start a family, but finding a dearth of eligible men, these women resign themselves to living alone as their biological clocks tick ever so much louder with each passing year.

And those men who are ready and eager to embrace the responsibility of being a loving husband and father often find the women in their lives suffering from sexual shame in their past or the trauma of a broken father relationship, which in turn affects all their relationships with men.

As a result, men and women are remaining single longer, and in some cases, never marry—in fact a recent study found a record number of never-married singles over the age of forty.[6] The result is many end up living a life of loneliness and disconnectedness as individuals.

This creates a demographic disaster for our society as there are not enough members of the younger generation to replace those who have retired from the workforce or passed away, or to provide the tax base for expensive entitlement programs, many of which were implemented in the 1960s, for older generations.

Thus, we are experiencing ever-rising national debt with a day of reckoning coming that will result in devastating economic consequences.

Our educational system is irreparably broken with major ramifications for all aspects of our culture and future as individuals and as a nation.

Families are caught in an endless cycle of generational poverty—trapping children, and their children, in a world with little or no hope of escape.

Spiritually, we are adrift. The common moral values we endorsed—if not always followed—as a nation are gone. In fact, what used to be deemed right is now wrong and vice versa. Drug use, such as marijuana and some hallucinogens, are now legal in order to benefit state treasuries. The old mainline churches many of us grew up in are closing by the thousands each year, and denominations are at war with each other over what used to be considered clear-cut biblical issues, particularly regarding human sexuality.

The result is a dispirited and divided America. Neighbors are pitted against neighbors, and in many cases, family members are pitted against other family members. Children no longer speak to their parents unless the mom and dad affirm every decision the child makes or embrace their "woke" ideology, or some parents reject their children if they do not see eye to eye on every issue. The result is increasing isolation as we hunker down in our various tribes warring with each other—sometimes under the same roof.

Our cities are burning, our social media is toxic, and, despite all good intentions, we are more splintered than ever before. The events of 2020—between COVID shutdowns and unfortunate and tragic incidents in our inner cities—threw gasoline on the smoldering fire under the cauldron. Many poor sections of our inner cities continue to decline, despite billions of dollars spent on so-called improvements, never improving anything. Crime continues to skyrocket as does homelessness. Urbanites belittle and despise rural Americans, and the feeling is mutual.

We have become a nation of blame-assigning finger-pointers—a nation with seemingly no hope that only wants to humiliate and defeat perceived enemies, rather than come together in shared unity.

We have become the antithesis of the utopian dream of John Lennon's "Imagine." But like so many other efforts to create a utopian society, a dystopian one, filled with suffering and injustice, was created instead.

So, how did we get here, and what is my answer to the reoccurring question I am asked? "What happened to America?"

The answer is simply: "The latest attempt to create utopia has failed: the 1960s."

It was in the 1960s that America discarded its fundamental underpinnings of faith, family, and respect, and our nation has never been the same since. Our relations with each other across every conceivable spectrum have only worsened, our inner cities have become more decayed, our educational system increasingly inept, our families splintered, and our national civility anything but.

As Kevin Boyle titled his book on the era, *The Shattering: America in the 1960s*,[7] our society is in shards. Or in the words of Robert O. Self, the history professor from Brown University quoted at the beginning, it was the decade when "Americans went to war with one another."[8]

And we have been at war with each other ever since, with the hope of a ceasefire growing dimmer and dimmer. Worse yet, the war is both internal and external.

Looking externally, according to the Brennan Center for Justice, the violent crime rate increased by 126 percent between 1960 and 1970, with the chance of being murdered doubling between 1964 and 1974.[9]

But the war we are experiencing reaches beyond external risks. The cultural impact goes far deeper, taking a toll emotionally, spiritually, and economically on our national psyche. That is the internal war we face.

What happened in the 1960s, and continues to this day, did not occur overnight. It was the culmination of incremental efforts by determined progressives to remake America into something the Founding Fathers would not recognize.

While much of America was unaware, in the first sixty years of the twentieth century, progressives were taking over every major institution: academia, religion, primary education, entertainment, and local governments. Once entrenched, they used raw power, ridicule, and intimidation to consolidate and strengthen their control.

At last, they could then launch their radical transformation in the 1960s—starting on the coasts, and like a bad cancer, eventually metastasizing inland. And like a spreading disease, America began eating away at itself until eventually nothing was left except an empty shell of what she once was.

In the 1960s, deviancy became exalted while normalcy became mocked. The so-called "counterculture" became the dominant culture, and the dominant culture either acquiesced or went into hiding. America has never been the same, with 1968 serving as the defining year when America's woven tapestry—which had been fraying throughout the 1960s—totally came apart.

In 1968, Rev. Dr. Martin Luther King Jr. and Robert Kennedy were assassinated. Radicalized college students ran amuck on campuses and draft cards were burned. Militant feminists demanded legalized abortion and race riots were seemingly happening in every major city.

America got a prime-time view of all the chaos when millions watched in horror as riots surged outside the Democratic National Convention in Chicago, resulting in more than 650 arrests. America's previously civil society had come apart at the seams.

As Jules Witcover would later write, "[1968 became the] pivotal year [when] something vital died—the post–World War II dream of an America that at last would face up to its most basic problems at home and abroad with wisdom, honesty, and compassion."[10]

The year 1968 also marked a significant setback in American efforts to achieve piece in Vietnam as the Tet Offensive, launched by North Vietnam against the South, threw gas on the smoldering fire that had been the Vietnam War, turning it into a raging fire that consumed our land and help lead to the end of Lyndon Johnson's presidency. Kenneth Walsh wrote about 1968 to say:

> Month after unsettling month, it became increasingly clear that America was losing its moorings, and no one knew where it would end. Adding to the concerns about violence and racial polarization, a generation gap had emerged between parents and their children over issues of war and peace, race, gender, sexual promiscuity, religion, patriotism, and lifestyle. This generational divide became one of the defining features of the period. College kids became increasingly disaffected with the establishment and, on campus, many demanded a more relevant curriculum and more student control over their own lifestyles and how their colleges and universities were being run. Feminism was on the march. A "counterculture" bloomed in which young people defied tradition and experimented with unconventional lifestyles marked in many cases by sexual promiscuity, drug use and confronting authority.[11]

Steven M. Gillon, a professor of history at the University of Oklahoma summarized 1968 powerfully, stating:

> Two assassinations, a bloody war, violent protests, racial unrest, colorful hippies, a celebration of sex and rebellion, and John Lennon's countercultural anthem, "Revolution"—1968 had them all. It was the year that shattered the fragile consensus that had shaped American society since the end of World War II. It was the year when assassinations ended the last hope of a nonviolent civil-rights movement and the

creation of a new biracial political coalition. The year witnessed the coming of age of the baby-boom generation, the 76 million Americans born between 1946 and 1964, who rebelled against tradition and all forms of conformity. And it forged, for better or worse, the world in which we live today. . . . Now, five decades later, despite all the changes that have taken place, the nation remains trapped in this ongoing struggle for the hearts and minds of the American people. We are still living in the long shadow of 1968.[12]

But 1968 was just the culmination of a long-standing effort by progressives to fundamentally change America and would only be the beginning of America's version of the Cold War in which we could become divided as a nation, ideologically, spiritually, and eventually geographically. In many ways, it has never ended.

While we have had brief interludes of perceived unity such as the 1980s and the days after September 11, 2001, at best, we have just been patching the holes in our national tapestry ever since—with some of the holes, in particular on moral and spiritual issues, growing larger and larger over time.

The revolutionaries who brought us 1968 would continue moving into the school boards, government, academia, entertainment, and all other aspects of American life while the majority of Americans—the ones Richard Nixon titled "The Silent Majority"—repelled by what they saw, tried to catch a collective breath and recover some sort of normalcy.

But that normalcy never returned. Thanks to the 1960s, even decades later, we find ourselves in a cultural, political, and spiritual mess that continues to pit left vs. right, religious vs. non-religious, men vs. women, gun control advocates vs.

gun owners, pacifists vs. military—all in a zero-sum game neither side can win.

The 1960s, and particularly 1968, may have come and gone in the annals of history, but its legacy continues to this day—and in fact, much of what we are experiencing now can be traced back to its poisonous roots.

As federal judge J. Harvie Wilkinson puts it, "The Sixties seemed to offer no life after death. No middle age. No life after tomorrow. No yesterdays. Only here and now, this compressed second, running on fumes. Time sliced from both ends to this screaming instant, this frantic sliver of sensation, for someone to shoot up and screech off in."[13]

In the 1960s, America replaced hope with despair, unity with division, and civility with hatred.

And the impact of the 1960s has been profound—and placed America on an increasingly slippery slope toward rejecting the values that first strengthened it into a beacon of light to the rest of the world. It was a cultural earthquake, not only exposing old fault lines but creating new ones that continue to shake us to our core.

For example, a 2023 *Wall Street Journal*/NORC poll found only 38 percent of respondents said patriotism was important to them, and only 39 percent said religion was very important. These numbers are sharply down from 70 percent and 62 percent respectively just twenty-five years ago. And only 23 percent of young adults under thirty said patriotism was very important and 31 percent cited religion as very important.[14]

Had those numbers been true in the 1940s, Adolf Hitler would have been sitting in the White House by early 1943.

The value of parenthood and having children dropped from 59 percent saying it was very important to them to just 30 percent in 2023. Community involvement dropped from 62 percent to 27 percent. But the importance of money rose from 31 percent to 43 percent.[15]

These numbers reflect the ethos of the 1960s continuing to erode each of these key areas over time. This ethos was a constant and annoying drip in our society and is quickly growing to a flood, washing away the values and principles that made America the greatest and freest nation on earth.

In their attempt to create their utopian dream, as I stated earlier, progressives turned America into a dystopian nightmare.

That is why I felt compelled to write this book. So many people are awakening to the fact our country is not what it used to be and are alarmed about where it is going. However, they have no idea how we got to this place and, sadly, often choose to engage in behaviors that only exacerbate, rather than heal, the problem.

I was born in January 1964 shortly after the assassination of President John F. Kennedy in November 1963, and just as Lyndon Johnson was taking office and beginning to make his great promises for what he would call the "Great Society."

I was one of the last of the "baby boomers"—the children born to the justly named "Greatest Generation" who survived the Great Depression and World War II.

Those 10–15 years older than I still have memories of America before the cultural earthquake that was the 1960s. The stories they've told me of America before the progressives took control, describe a simpler time—not without faults, especially with regard to civil rights—where Americans respected each other, had reverence for God, and were unified in national purpose.

My friend Bobb Biehl says, and accurately, "Nothing has meaning without context." This book is meant to provide that context, so you, the reader, can understand what the progressive Left sought to do, treating America like the proverbial frog in a pot, slowly turning up the heat until it boils to death. But it is also meant to provide hope—to illustrate how we can put the 1960s in the rearview mirror and move forward as a united, rather than a divided, nation. Understanding the past also provides us with a roadmap to the future. If we are to build a future recapturing America's past glory and reversing the damage of the 1960s, we have to study the tactics of those who successfully implemented their agenda while America was asleep. No battle can be won without doing some reconnaissance first.

One of my dearest friends grew up in Northern California, where the beginning stages of the 1960s' upheaval manifested. As a child raised there, he had a unique firsthand look. He provided me with his observations—from his childhood to the present day—through a series of letters to a hypothetical pen pal in the Midwest, telling me how the 1960s transformed his once-conservative small town over a nearly sixty-year period.

What he provided is a fascinating commentary, from an eyewitness perspective, of the devastation of the 1960s on our social fabric and his life. I have chosen to start the book with what he wrote as I believe it provides a vivid picture of what the 1960s launched and continues to inflict upon our land.

That said, I do want to state our nation was not perfect before this turbulent decade, and there were some *positive* developments in the 1960s. It was the decade America finally came to grips with the racism of our past through the civil rights movement. For that we can be thankful. Individuals such as the Rev. Dr. Martin Luther King Jr. are to be commended for finally bringing this national sin to light and forcing many Americans to confront and overcome their past actions toward the African American community. There is still much healing to be done, but at least Dr. King's efforts opened a national dialogue that ended the denial of the scourge of racism in our midst.

It was the decade when we put a man on the moon and heard Neil Armstrong declare, "One small step for man, one giant leap for mankind,"[16] as he set foot on the lunar surface on July 20, 1969.

So amidst the darkness of the 1960s, there were still moments of light—moments that inspired and bettered the world.

Ultimately, my goal is to provide hope, not just heap on another helping of despair on America's overflowing plate but instead provide a roadmap for a unified future. The damage of the 1960s is not irreversible, but it will take time and perseverance to slowly reclaim each institution the progressive Left captured during the twentieth century.

I am an eternal optimist, and I believe we can make America once again the "shining city on a hill" for which Ronald Reagan so eloquently advocated. I believe we can leave a legacy for future generations to enjoy such that when they are asked, "What happened to America?" they can respond, "She threw off the shackles of the 1960s and is moving forward into a glorious future."

That is the utopia I hope and pray for.

Tim Goeglein
Washington, DC

CHAPTER ONE

Letters from a
Pen Pal

Belaboring [the 60s] now might seem like flogging a dead horse. But large, ingrained, intergenerational social pathologies such as homelessness and underclass culture don't spring up overnight from trivial causes. They are the seed sown by the Haves and rooted years ago. We can't help but cure them without knowing what caused and furthered them—and continues to further them even now.[1]

—Myron Magnet

To many, however, the Sixties were marked by the worst of baby boomer self-indulgence, and the decade certainly didn't achieve the counterculture's objectives of ending poverty, war, and intolerance. In some ways, the decade had quite the opposite effect, igniting a culture war that turned virulent and that persists in some ways today.[2]

—Kenneth Walsh

April 1965

Dear Pen Pal:

In your previous letter, you asked me about the town I live in.

Our small town is located in Northern California. It's really a nice place. The downtown area has wonderful old buildings, tree-lined streets, and no crime whatsoever. We live on a nice quiet street where I get to play with my friends, and we rarely worry about locking our doors. We also like to ride our bicycles around the neighborhood. The only thing I am afraid of is a dog that likes to chase after me and bark when I ride down his street. I try to avoid him.

I am really looking forward to the yearly parade in town in a few days. People are so proud of our city and country. The marching bands, military veterans, and the other civic groups that march in the parade really bring us together as a community. This summer we have a county fair with fun rides and the local dairy handing out free ice cream.

I love going to the neighborhood candy store that is run by an elderly couple. The other day, I went there with my 25-cent allowance. I picked out my candy and handed the man a quarter. I didn't realize I had to pay sales tax, and I thought I might have to put something back. But he smiled and told me it was OK. That was so nice of him.

My dad took me to lunch downtown yesterday. It was fun. The men were all wearing suits and ties, and the women were in nice dresses. I had a grilled cheese sandwich. It was delicious. It's so wonderful to see how polite everyone is.

We start each day at school saying the Pledge of Allegiance and singing "My Country 'Tis of Thee." I enjoy that. It makes me feel proud to be an American.

We go to the local Methodist church on Sundays. I have to get all dressed up for that. I really don't listen to the

sermon much, but everyone is so kind to each other that I
enjoy my time there anyway.
I hope that answers your question! I look forward to
hearing about your town.

Sincerely,

Your Pen Pal

Five years later . . . (1970)

Dear Pen Pal:

There is so much going on and so much is changing. I'm
not sure what to make of it all.
Our Sunday school class is putting on a play at the local
Methodist church. It is about protesting the Vietnam War
and social injustice. We were told we should be angry and
organize protests. I keep wondering what this all had to do
with God.
There's also a lot of people fighting in our church, and
many are thinking of leaving because they do not like the
political direction the church is taking. My father is particularly vocal about it, and it makes me sad. Our family is
divided over it. I'm getting a bit disillusioned by it all. I
don't enjoy going to church at all anymore.
Our hometown parade was last week. A lot of anti-war
protestors were there yelling for us to get out of Vietnam.
When the military veterans marched by, some people booed
and yelled bad words at them. Some folks in the crowd held
signs promoting smoking marijuana, and I could smell a
strange odor in the air.
We started singing a new song at school, "If I Had a
Hammer." It seems a little angry to me. We aren't singing

"My Country 'Tis of Thee" anymore. That makes me sad too.

I'm finding out things about my classmates in fifth grade that I wish I didn't know. I found out that a few of them are using drugs. Something else to be sad about.

Our town has really changed. I don't think it is for the better.

Sincerely,

Your Pen Pal

Five years later . . . (1975)

Dear Pen Pal:

Gosh, it's hard to believe I'll be starting high school soon. I'm so glad to be getting out of junior high. Every day, I'm just glad to come out alive. We have gangs that intimidate you and threaten to beat you up. Three of our cheerleaders got beaten up by one gang who ripped the earrings out of their ears. Ouch! One of our teachers got beat up by some guys who came on campus to cause trouble. I don't feel safe, and there are days I go to school trembling in fear.

We got some new ministers at church. They told us that we should reject the patriarchy and pray to Mother God. The church also wants us to attend a sex ed course that is taught by a group called Planned Parenthood. I quit going to the youth group because it was more about sex than it was about God. I heard that a lot of things going on there seemed more like an R-rated movie than a church youth group.

In my world history class, I'm told our country is evil. My teacher has pictures of Lenin and Mao hanging up on the wall, and he likes to talk about how wonderful they are while talking about how corrupt our nation is. This is so different from the history I learned in elementary school. Back then, my teachers said our founding fathers were heroes. Now, I'm being told that all they wanted to do was enslave people and force their religion on them.

My parents told me the other day that they don't want me going downtown by myself because they don't think it is safe anymore. Not even our neighborhood is anymore. The kid next door got high on drugs, got into his father's car, and crashed it into the house across the street.

I hope things are better in your town because things aren't good here.

Sincerely,

Your Pen Pal

Four years later . . . (1979)

Dear Pen Pal:

It's been a hard year. I started community college in the fall.

In my film study class, the instructor brought in a friend who showed us his hardcore pornographic films. We had no warning about what we were about to be subjected to. I was trapped, but finally found a way to leave between films so I did not have to watch anymore.

Earlier this year, on our band tour, one of my bandmates opened up an entire shoebox of marijuana joints on the bus and started handing them out like candy. Practically the whole bus lit up, except me. They even convinced the bus driver to take a puff. All I could do was silently suffer through it all. This is so against how I was brought up. I'm very depressed.

Speaking of depressed, I just found that one of my former classmates, Cheryl, overdosed on drugs and died. She used to sit next to me in English, and we played in the band together. She was a sweet girl, but the last time I saw her I could tell something was seriously wrong. I have no idea what would have led her to do something like that, but I heard that her parents had gotten a divorce, and she was forced to move away from her friends. Six months later, she decided to take her own life. It is so sad.

Then the other day, another of my friends, Steve, from Boy Scouts, while high on drugs, took out a gun and blew his brains out in front of his girlfriend. I am going to his service on Monday. It is really hard to understand why all of this is happening. Things seemed so much more innocent when I was a child. Did I just never know this all was going on?

We had Easter services at church last Sunday. Instead of hearing about Christ, we were told it was our Christian duty to protest at the Livermore Nuclear Labs because they're "an assault on creation."

My father, who works in title insurance, told our family the other night at dinner that no one can buy a home right now because inflation and interest rates are so high. He says he feels so bad for young families trying to start out these days because they are facing the double whammy of inflation and recession. He called it "stagflation."

Things are so different from my childhood. There are times when I wonder how things changed so quickly, but then I think back to what happened around 1967–68. And the reason things changed becomes much clearer.

All I ask myself is, "Will this nightmare ever end?"

Sincerely,

Your Pen Pal

Thirty-nine years later . . . (2018)

Dear Pen Pal:

Remember when I wrote years ago, asking, "Will this nightmare ever end?"
It hasn't.
I returned to my hometown last weekend for a high school reunion. It's so sad. The downtown, which was once so beautiful, is littered with tents for countless homeless people who have no place to live. When you walk the streets, you see human feces, vomit, and drug paraphernalia on every corner. I struggled not to cry. I remember when everything was so different. Many of my friends and family who live there want to escape but feel trapped. What is ironic is that they voted for and supported the policies of the people who created this mess.
It's hard to believe this is the idyllic little town I knew as a child, but it's the logical culmination of everything I saw happen during my teenage years in the 1960s and 1970s. It's a tragedy, and my heart is grieved.

Sincerely,

Your Pen Pal

Five years later (2023)

Dear Pen Pal:

I was back in my hometown for another class reunion. It was good to see a lot of my old classmates.
Our reunion was downtown. A homeless man screamed obscenities at me as my wife and I walked by. I won't repeat

what he was calling me. My focus was zeroed in on keeping my wife safe because I was afraid he was going to attack us both at any moment.

The downtown is still a mess and is nothing more than rows of marijuana dispensaries, tattoo shops, and New Age bookstores, paired with people openly engaging in drug use. My friends continue to talk about how bad it all is, but they seemingly have no idea how to make things better, and they keep supporting the policies that first created this mess. It will require tremendous effort to reverse what's been done, but perhaps no longer being in denial about the damage started in the 1960s is a start.

Sincerely,

Your Pen Pal

In reading over my friend's observations, it is easy to ask: How did things change so drastically between 1965 and 1969? How did this once-idyllic small town become a place people now want to avoid?

The answer, as I stated in my introduction, is the radical and rapid transformation of America that transpired in the 1960s.

The activists who transformed America were hoping to turn it into a leftist utopia of free love, socialism, and secularism. Much of it started in Northern California where my friend grew up. He saw firsthand what we were all to experience later.

Now, sixty years later, instead of being a "shining city on a hill," America is known more for out-of-wedlock births, out-of-control government spending, rotting bureaucratic infrastructure, shootings, and increasing division and hostility toward each other.

So how did we get to the 1960s? Let's start by entering what Mr. Peabody called the "Wayback Machine" and return to the early days of the twentieth century and the birth of the progressive movement—with its corrupt vehicle that set America down the road to a destructive decade.

CHAPTER TWO

How the Stumbling Began

The Left doesn't admit being wrong. It merely sloughs off causes quietly and moves on to new bogus ventures. These unwanted cultural, social, and economic novelties then, as surely as night follows day, are exposed as unfounded, unworkable, and dangerous.[1]

—Hugh Gordon

Sixty years ago, there were no culture wars as we know them today. Yes, people disagreed with each other, as they have since the dawn of history, but neighbors were, for the most part, civil to each other, regardless of their religious or political differences. Communities were proud and pitched in together for the common good, with no one demanding special privileges or affirmation of every personal decision.

Then the 1960s arrived, and Americans turned on each other with a vengeance. Despite the appearance of societal bliss in the decades preceding the 1960s, seeds of destruction that would lead to the ripping apart of our national tapestry were planted decades before.

The seeds leading to the blooming1960s were planted at the turn of the twentieth century with the so-called "progressive movement" led by individuals such as John Dewey, Margaret Sanger, Roger Baldwin, and President Woodrow Wilson. To comprehend the 1960s, you need to understand the genesis and goals of the progressive movement and how they slowly and steadily took over every vital American institution—government, education, entertainment, and commerce.

The ideas of the 1960s also emerged from a radicalized academia and the philosophies of Karl Marx, Friedrich Engels, Herbert Marcuse, Friedrich Nietzsche, John Dewey (much more on him shortly), and others. At the turn of the century, groups such as the American Civil Liberties Union (ACLU) and Planned Parenthood came into being.

Marx and Engels were the creators of communism, which had a powerful influence on the progressive movement. For instance, Engels argued, using the anthropological evidence of his time, family structures changed over history, and the concept of monogamous marriage arose from the necessity created by class systems for men to control women to ensure their own children would inherit their property. It's easy to see how Engels's argument was weaponized to attack traditional family structure and values, and communism contributed a great deal more ammunition through similar theories and propositions.

Marcuse's Marxist scholarship inspired many radical intellectuals and political activists in the 1960s and 1970s, in the United States and internationally. His focus was on human sexuality because he believed the "realization" of man's erotic nature would result in the true liberation of humanity. One of his most prominent works, a book titled *Eros and Civilization,* offered a Neo-Freudian view of man. The book claimed tolerance toward sexuality and eroticism would create a better life. This book made Marcuse one of the most significant philosophers of the "sexual revolution."[2] He also became known as the "Father of the New Left."

It was Nietzsche who proclaimed, "God is dead"[3] and whose teachings would become an inspiration to Adolf Hitler and the Nazi Party. He lapsed into insanity before he died,[4] but his anti-religious and anti-God philosophies and rejection of all moral principles and objective truth, called "nihilism," would become prevalent among the most radical of the 1960s' activists.

At the turn of the century the so-called "social justice" movement started to creep into mainline religious denominations, utopian visions such as the League of Nations were born, and the theory of evolution started to be promoted to supplant the traditional understanding that God created the heavens and the earth. Slowly, but surely, the progressive movement started to question, and eventually remove, faith's role in the public square, replacing faith with their secular and godless reality.

It was a multi-decade-long chipping away process that weakened America's moral foundations to the point our nation's walls would eventually start to crumble and finally collapse in the 1960s. While trying to create a progressive utopia, these activists stumbled into creating a slum instead.

Utopians such as John Dewey designed the public education system to shape young minds to accept progressive dogma as truth from an early age. Universities, many originally established by Christians, rejected their religious foundations as progressive academics rose to positions of power.

The entertainment industry, especially with the advent of motion pictures, launched a celebration of vice over virtue, at least until the Production Code of 1934 reined it in for the next thirty years. But then, the Production Code was scrapped, and a Pandora's box of graphic sex and violence was unleased in American theaters and on television.

The expansion of the federal government into a national nanny on a perpetual spending binge began in earnest during this period as well.

Roger Baldwin, founder of the ACLU in 1920, was a notable leader among those who sought to radically change America. Baldwin described himself as agnostic and socialist, with Communist leanings. Baldwin was heavily influenced by his grandfather, who viewed himself as an "anti-Christian crusader." Among Baldwin's associates were Planned Parenthood founder Margaret Sanger, radical anarchist Emma Goldman, and Russian anarchist Prince Peter Alexeyevich Kropotkin.

In a biography based on personal interviews with Roger Baldwin, Peggy Lamson wrote, "[Kropotkin's] espousal of anarchism was based on the belief that true cooperation between human beings would make government rule superfluous. His utopia would come into being, he believed, when neither private property nor the church nor the state exercised control over the individual spontaneity of man."[5]

It is this philosophy we now see played out in current American society, and it came into full bloom in the 1960s with chants such as "Not the church, not the state, only I will decide my fate." We live in a society that took root in the 1960s and celebrates Kropotkin's and Baldwin's desires to banish control over the "individual spontaneity of man." Thus, our new cultural mantras are "you do you" or "if it feels good, do it," regardless of how it impacts others. In this new world, man becomes his own god.

This new movement based on radical individualism called itself "progressives" and rejected the first principles upon which our nation was founded—our rights come from God, and not from man.

And that rejection of God, unleashed all manner of evil—as we have seen throughout human history going back to Adam and Eve in the garden of Eden.

As Baldwin put it in his thirtieth anniversary Harvard University class book,

> I am for socialism, disarmament, and ultimately the abolishing of the state itself as an instrument of violence and compulsion. I seek social ownership of all property, the abolition of the propertied class, and sole control of those who produce wealth. Communism is the goal.[6]

As we will see, Baldwin's philosophies, along with the others mentioned, germinated and reached fruition in the 1960s.

WOODROW WILSON

Besides Roger Baldwin and the ACLU, perhaps the most important figure in ushering in the Progressive movement—and its destructive policies in the 1960s—was President Woodrow Wilson. Wilson in his utopianism laid the groundwork for the later rejection of constitutional originalism and the massive expansion of the federal government, climaxing with the destructive Great Society programs implemented by President Lyndon Johnson in the mid-1960s.

Wilson entered politics from a career in academia where, as president of Princeton University, he created a system that eventually became the model for bloated higher education bureaucracy that persists to this day. Elected as governor of New Jersey in 1910, the ambitious Wilson coveted the idea of becoming president, and thanks to a unique set of circumstances, he got his wish.

Wilson was elected to the presidency in 1912 when former President Theodore Roosevelt and his hand-picked successor and then-current President William Howard Taft had a particularly nasty falling out—resulting in Roosevelt running as the third party "Bull Moose" candidate, thus dividing the Republican vote and enabling Wilson's win.

Up until Wilson's election, the Democratic Party had not held the White House since Grover Cleveland, whose second term ended in 1897 and who was conservative in his policies—so much so his party pre-empted his run to retain the presidency in 1898 by nominating the progressive William Jennings Bryan in place of the incumbent president. Repeated presidential election losses left Democrats desperate to find a nominee to replace William Jennings Bryan, who repeatedly lost the general election to Republicans: McKinley (twice) and Taft. Wilson was chosen as a fresh face to replace the thrice-unsuccessful Bryan whose constituency came from agrarian rather than urban America.

Just like Ross Perot divided the vote in 1992, leading to the election of Bill Clinton over George H. W. Bush, and George Wallace's 1968 candidacy likely handed the presidency to Richard Nixon, Theodore Roosevelt's candidacy ensured a Wilson victory—a victory that would ultimately do irreparable damage to America on many levels and sent the Democratic Party down the progressive path it's followed ever since. It also started the Democratic Party's shift to an urban party instead of a rural party, which eventually delivered rural voters to the Republicans decades later.

Even though he had no mandate to speak of, as he was beneficiary of the Republican split more than anything else, Wilson, like many progressives before and since, governed like he had a powerful mandate and went to work implementing his agenda almost immediately—an agenda most people, had they been aware of it, might have been unlikely to support.

The first "reform" instituted by Wilson was the explosive growth of government, and the institution of what has become known as the "imperial presidency." It was Wilson who signed the Federal Reserve Act, which created a

Socialist-style central planning of the economy and gave politicians a blank check to spend government money without concern for financial backing.[7]

Thus, the origin of our current $33 trillion, and growing, national debt can be traced back to the policies of the Wilson administration. And the debt exploded under future progressive presidents such as Franklin Roosevelt and Lyndon Johnson, with the latter throwing gasoline on the fiscal fire with his Great Society programs of the 1960s.

But beyond promoting fiscal irresponsibility and crippling taxation, what was perhaps most alarming about Wilson was his disregard and, in many cases, contempt for America's founders and the U.S. Constitution. It is this philosophy which would eventually spread throughout America's elite law schools as progressives seized control—turning American courts into policy-making bodies in place of their original purpose as interpreters, not makers, of law.

Ronald J. Pestritto, the graduate dean and professor of politics at Hillsdale College, writes:

> While volumes of biographies have been filled with details of Wilson's life—and especially of his time in public service—it was Wilson's political ideas that made the most lasting mark on American political life. These are ideas that helped to shape the profound challenge offered by the Progressive Movement to the basic political principles that undergirded the American constitutional order.[8]

Pestritto adds that Wilson's form of progressivism was designed to present a rationale for moving beyond the political thinking of the American Founding. One of the concepts most critical for this shift was the reinvention of the U.S. Constitution, which was declared to be "a living document" designed to adapt and conform to societal norms.

Especially in the 1960s, the political Left began to use this theory to shape and stretch the Constitution into a document none of the founders would have recognized.

This new legal approach reached full bloom in the Supreme Court during the Earl Warren court of the 1960s. This dismal blooming led to the end of school prayer and the creation of the "right to privacy" via "emanations" from "the penumbra" (whatever that means) from various amendments to the U.S. Constitution,[9] and it eventually resulted in legalized abortion and other rights that as Chief Justice John Roberts would write, "has no basis in the Constitution"[10] as well as the expansion of government into previously untouched areas.

Pestritto wrote:

> This interpretation of the Founding ran up against the Founders' own self-understanding, as Wilson well knew. This is why much of his scholarship is devoted to a radical reinterpretation and critique of the political theory of the Founding. Wilson understood that the limits placed upon the power of the national government by the Constitution—limits that Progressives wanted to see relaxed if not removed—were grounded in the natural-rights principles of the Declaration of Independence. This meant, for Wilson, that both the Declaration and the Constitution had to be understood anew through a Progressive lens.[11]

In fact, in 1911, Wilson said, "the rhetorical introduction of the Declaration of Independence is the least part of it. . . If you want to understand the real Declaration of Independence, do not repeat the preface."[12] In other words, the Declaration's foundational statements about equality and natural rights should be disregarded.

This view was rapidly adopted by academia, Wilson's home turf as the former president of Princeton University and was first promoted and implemented there. From academic circles, this position leaked back into society as "expert" opinion that would deeply impact society in the 1960s and ever after.

But beyond his contempt for the Preamble to the Declaration of Independence, Wilson also disdained the U.S. Constitution—particularly its insistence on the separation of powers.

In fact, when he ran for governor of New Jersey, he pledged to become an "unconstitutional governor," meaning he had no intent to adhere to the role outlined for the chief executive under the state constitution's separation of powers.[13]

Wilson stands as a precursor of the impending popular mindset whose policies would actually create more poverty and more despair under the guise of "helping" and "social justice." Wilson felt the separation of powers was designed to unnecessarily protect people from themselves. He believed the system, as set up by the founders, created obstacles that formed barriers to implementing the "will of the people."

What Wilson and others did not consider was the system's checks and balances, as set up by the Founding Fathers, were intended to create mutual accountability between the federal government's three branches and to ensure policies directly impacting American citizens would be well thought out and thoroughly debated.

Wilson laid the groundwork for what was to come through blurring the clearly defined roles between the executive, legislative, and judicial branches. This erosion of governmental roles enabled progressives to circumvent the American constitutional system to achieve their aims, with their efforts culminating in the political, judicial, and social upheaval of the 1960s.

As we will see, discarding the separation of powers and parceling out decision making to various agencies, with competing interests and ideologies, resulted (and continues to result) in the rise of a politically elite class whose edicts and mandates often harm the American people rather than helped them.

Rather than Congress setting policies, dependent on the approval or veto of the executive branch and subject to constitutional review by the judicial branch, unaccountable federal agencies have run amuck. Thus, we now have agencies making decisions and decrees, often without thorough consideration, which have taken a wrecking ball to many a small business and raised prices on many goods and services to the point they are no longer accessible for large segments of the American population.

In the 1960s, Lyndon Johnson put the Woodrow Wilson agenda on steroids, resulting in the stifling regulation culture we experience today.

A classic example is the current bureaucratic effort to force all Americans into electric cars, which are far more expensive to purchase and maintain, and thus denying lower income and middle-class citizens who do not live in urban centers with mass transit systems needed access to an essential form of transportation allowing them to travel, work, and potentially move upward economically.

Many government regulations, even needed ones, are no longer made by leaders whom voters can hold accountable. Instead, these decisions are made by bureaucrats who can impose their personal agendas without facing the consequences of their actions directly with the voters they're regulating.

The disdain Wilson and other progressive thinkers of his day felt for the U.S. Constitution, laid the foundation for what we are experiencing today. The explosive growth of government, as we will see, created policies that exacerbated poverty, impeded societal progress, and actually widened the gap between the haves and have-nots.

In addition, new "rights," none of which are mentioned in the Constitution, are often forced upon Americans through government agencies, rather than through robust debate and legislative action. Thus, as the Wilsonian philosophy began to take root in numerous aspects of culture throughout the 1920s and beyond, many Americans lost their right to raise their children without government interference, were told what faith practices were approved or disapproved of, and faced punishment, both economic and social, if they did not comply with the mandates coming from unaccountable elites in government agencies.

H. L. Mencken, a liberal journalist and social critic, wrote on the eve of the 1920 election that Americans were sickened of Wilsonian "idealism that is oblique, confusing, dishonest, and ferocious."[14] Many Americans are still sick of it today, because this idealism was embraced and implemented by progressives in the 1960s.

So why is this all important? Because even though Wilson's philosophies (and those of the progressive movement) may have been rejected by the American people when first introduced at the beginning of the century, these philosophies didn't disappear. Rather, they slowly took over every major institution of American society—from academia to public education to entertainment and so forth—until they exploded into the cultural upheaval of the 1960s and beyond.

And as previously mentioned, the massive expansion of the federal government—and its intrusive regulation of American lives—was put in place through the Johnson administration's Great Society reforms and the creation of numerous additional federal agencies during the 1960s. The result: a less free, more regulated, and increasingly divided America.

THE PORT HURON STATEMENT AND THE LAUNCH OF THE PROTEST MOVEMENT

The watershed moment leading to the full launch of the 1960s' transformation of America occurred on June 15, 1962, when the *Port Huron Statement* (written by Tom Hayden, a member of the infamous "Chicago Seven" and the future husband of actress Jane Fonda) was released by radical activist college students associated with Students for a Democratic Society (SDS). The sexual revolution, radical feminism, the corruption of the arts, and the modish disrespect for America were birthed through this statement.

As Al Mohler wrote, "If you want to understand the ideological controversies behind today's headlines, you need to look to the past—and to one specific event . . . the Port Huron Statement. . . . It is now clear that those students and their political allies were not only ambitious—they were successful. America, as we know it today, has been reshaped by the ideas and energies of the New Left—and the revolution continues."[15]

All the groundwork laid by progressive activists throughout the twentieth century would be summarized and demanded by Hayden and SDS in the statement: sexual revolution, radical feminism, liberal takeover of academia, defunding and dismantling of the U.S. military, government takeover of private enterprise, universal health care, abolishment of prisons, demonization of the views and values of rural America, international control—via the United Nations—of public education, and the radicalization of the arts and other cultural institutions to advance and implement progressive ideology throughout American society.

One item of particular note we now see played out daily in America, is the statement's call for teachers' unions to be politicized and used to push for "progressive change" as well as for university employees "and thereby an important element in the education of the student radical."[16] In fact, the statement particularly pinpointed universities as the best opening for pushing their radical agenda, calling for an alliance of progressive students and faculty to seize control of university campuses.[17] It comes as no surprise then to see the current progressive domination of university campuses to indoctrinate youth and estrange them from their parents and their parents' views.

Meanwhile, at the K-12 level, today's teachers' unions are not concerned about children's education in comparison with their drive to seize control of children's hearts and minds from their parents. These teachers' unions engage in protest marches for progressive causes, and just about everything else, except education.

The *Port Huron Statement* also called for a "New Left" to stir controversy across the land, dividing Americans while pursuing their "reform agenda," which they stated would require union between traditional liberals and socialists.[18]

In addition, the statement condemned America's opposition to Fidel Castro's Communist regime, decrying America as being unjustly hostile to Castro and his "reforms."[19] It further railed against America's supposedly paranoid view of the Soviet Union as a barrier to "disarmament" and "peace," and it basically called for America to no longer defend itself against the Soviet threat and to cease supporting governments trying to stop Soviet expansionism.[20] History has proven, with the fall of the Soviet Union in the late-1980s/early-1990s, that peace through weakness was not an effective route.

In many ways, the progressives who wrote the *Port Huron Statement* felt Baldwin, Dewey, and others did not go *far enough* and acted too slowly in their incremental approach to social change. In fact, they saw them as failures. They wanted a faster and more radical takeover of every American institution and they set out to do so. They replaced the slow, incremental approach of the progressives with a movement fueled by cultural steroids.

As Mohler writes, "The SDS activists wanted what amounts to a Marxist revolution that would transform American society from top to bottom. . . . They supercharged Marxism with an even more Utopian vision."[21]

The SDS wanted what they called a "participatory democracy," in which every group could air their grievances and demand new rights, accusing American culture of robbing individuals of their "inner authenticity," by which they meant every individual, and not God, determines their destiny. Of course, there were carnal motives behind all this. In Mohler's words, "As history would reveal, the mostly white male college students [who wrote the statement] were more intent on getting their girlfriends into bed,"[22] and they needed a sexual revolution to destroy the societal taboos limiting their ability to do so.

And thanks to Kinsey, Masters and Johnson, and the pill (which we will discover in the next chapter), they had the arguments and means to satisfy their libidos.

But some of them were politically savvy and figured out how to cloak their agenda. As Hayden wrote, "We will be 'out' if we are explicitly socialists, or if we espouse any minority political views honestly. . . . We can be further 'in' if we are willing to call socialism 'liberalism.'"[23]

Hayden, while definitely a revolutionary, knew he had to work within the system, rather than against the system, to achieve the change he wanted. He would eventually become the husband of actress Jane Fonda, and as a California state senator he used the mechanisms of political power to achieve his aims.

Amity Shlaes writes, "From the moment the Port Huron Conference [which resulted in the *Port Huron Statement*] kicked off, the split between those willing to work within the great American political machine and those who want to work outside that machine made itself felt."[24] Thus, while many of the more radical activists would never gain true access to elected office, the ones, like Hayden, who knew how to press their agenda in a more palatable form did win elections and gain the accompanying political power.

By the late-1960s/early-1970s, these activists had severely disrupted American society to achieve their aims, and within a decade successfully entrenched themselves in power in government, education, academia, entertainment, and religion by labeling themselves "liberals." As my friend wrote to his hypothetical pen pal, the difference between his town in 1965 and 1970 was swift and startling.

While those who wrote the *Port Huron Statement* are now in their late seventies and early eighties, they raised a new generation of followers through the academia of the 1980s, 1990s, and 2000s, who, fueled by the sexual revolution, victimization, and contempt for American ideals, eventually led to the "woke" culture of the 2020s, where anything and anyone who does not embrace their progressive ideology is promptly "cancelled."

As Myron Magnet wrote, "The new adversary stance towards conventional beliefs and ideals, breathlessly reported by the press and diffused almost instantly among the young, quickly put traditional values on the defensive, making them newly problematic even for those who continue to hold them."[25] As I said earlier, right became wrong and wrong became right.

And unfortunately, the beliefs that came out of the white middle-to-upper class kids associated with groups such as the SDS, would be devastating for the working class they purported to help. These groups protested from a position of economic and social comfort that gave them leeway to recover from certain negative consequences, but the beliefs they promoted unleashed drugs, sexual promiscuity, and other negative influences upon the working class—trapping them in escalating poverty and despair.

Magnet wrote:

> When middle class college kids began their fling with "protest," drugs, sexual experimentation, and dropping out in the sixties, they had a margin of safety because of their class. Working class kids . . . run a bigger risk. Once they drop out, some may never get back in . . . devoid of skills, discipline, or direction, and most of them—along with many of the homeless nationwide—dependent on drugs, alcohol, or both.[26]

As Magnet conclude, "'Turn on, tune in, and drop out' was the slogan of the sixties' counterculture, and the underclass duly turned on."[27]

It is no coincidence, then, current American society is dealing with an epidemic of homelessness. Tent cities, open drug use, public urination and defecation, and rampant crime are impacting not only our urban centers but moving into small towns in rural areas as well.

These rural areas, many of which struggled for a long time to adhere to traditional values, have become islands of devastation, filled with drug abuse, economic ruin, and little hope. This destruction stems from the policies implemented at the state and federal level as the middle-to-upper class radicals of the 1960s have moved into positions of power. Many in rural America now hold those who forced these policies upon them in contempt, resulting in ever-rising anger and despair.

Author Roger L. Simon has written a rather damning indictment of the generation behind the *Port Huron Statement*, which contrary to popular belief, were not Baby

Boomers (those born after 1945) but the end of the previous generation known as the Builders (born from 1935–1945). Simon noted the "moral narcissism" of the Builder Generation, who were born directly after the "Greatest Generation"—the generation born between 1917–1934 and who survived the Great Depression and fought in World War II.

Simon writes, "[The Greatest Generation] should have been the ones to form the future, but as it happened, we were the ones. We overcame them to become the commissars of the American zeitgeist, the arbiters of all things cultural and consequently political. No one else has gotten in much of a word edgewise."[28]

Simon goes on to cite the birthdates of the radicals who transformed American society in the 1960s: cultural revolutionary John Lennon (1940), *Port Huron Statement* contributing writer Tom Hayden (1939), militant feminist Gloria Steinem (1934), anti-war activist Abbie Hoffman (1936), and the notorious pro-obscenity activist Allan Ginsberg (1926). He calls them the "Least-Great Generation" or "Maybe the Ungrateful Generation" or the "Generation of 1968."

He writes, "As the years rolled on and centuries turned, it became ever clearer that we were callow, even selfish, inside. . . . Worse than that, we had—consciously or unconsciously or both—worked to unwind everything our parents had built. And it had its result, although not all of us desired it—or were later surprised by what we had wrought."[29]

It is only natural when a society starts to turn its back on God, as America did in the 1960s, it would focus on self. It is also not a coincidence the radicals of the 1960s were born during the Great Depression era, when socialist ideals started their initial creep into American society through the New Deal entitlement programs of Franklin Roosevelt. The 1930s were also when the Soviet Union made penetrating inroads to American academia, science, media, and government. *Witness* by White Chambers is a salient read on this subject.

What is interesting to note is how the radicals of the 1960s who developed the *Port Huron Statement* soon became the "establishment" they rebelled so strongly against forty years before. These same radicals now rule school boards, state and local governments, and many mainline religious denominations, and they embrace the benefits of capitalism while restricting it to fit their agenda and making it more difficult for the lower and middle classes to survive their higher taxation and ever-increasing government regulation and mandates.

As the late Walt Kelly said in the comic strip *Pogo*, "We have met the enemy, and he is us."

Simon writes, "The Generation of '68 and its followers had gone mainstream, transmogrifying radical symbols into specific forms of conspicuous consumption. A trip to Whole Foods in a Tesla became the equivalent of striking a blow against world hunger."[30]

And just like they can't buy a Tesla to make rich, climate-change progressives happy, most low-income Americans can't afford to shop at Whole Foods either. The Port Huron radicals, who argued for a more equal and just society, instead created exactly the opposite—and the weight of despair that followed their destructive efforts.

SAUL ALINSKY AND *RULES FOR RADICALS*

But perhaps the most important player behind the social chaos of the 1960s that continues today was Chicago community organizer Saul Alinsky, who wrote *Rules for Radicals*, a book dedicated to the "original deceiver": Lucifer or Satan. Alinsky was also the subject of Hillary Clinton's honors thesis at Wellesley College.

In a 1972 interview in *Playboy* magazine, given shortly before his death, Alinsky engaged in the following exchange:

PLAYBOY: Having accepted your own mortality, do you believe in any kind of afterlife?

ALINSKY: Sometimes it seems to me that the question people should ask is not "Is there life after death?" but "Is there life after birth?" I don't know whether there's anything after this or not. I haven't seen the evidence one way or the other and I don't think anybody else has either. But I do know that man's obsession with the question comes out of his stubborn refusal to face up to his own mortality. Let's say that if there is an afterlife, and I have anything to say about it, I will unreservedly choose to go to hell.

PLAYBOY: Why?

ALINSKY: Hell would be heaven for me. All my life I've been with the have-nots. Over here, if you're a have-not, you're short of dough. If you're a have-not in hell, you're short of virtue. Once I get into hell, I'll start organizing the have-nots over there.

PLAYBOY: Why them?

ALINSKY: They're my kind of people.[31]

Wayne Laugesen writes: "Alinsky had bold and clear advice for progressives, long before Hillary Clinton interviewed him for her thesis and 25 years before publication of the now-famous *Rules for Radicals*. His suggested method was to attack opponents personally, intimidate them, disorient them, dissuade them, throw them off their game, and consider breaking their necks."[32] So much for civil discourse.

According to Laugesen, the FBI's Baltimore report included a copy of Alinsky's 1972 interview with *Playboy* magazine, in which he describes his connection with Capone and the status he earned as the Chicago mob's college-boy "mascot."

Laugesen adds how Alinsky worked his way into Capone's circle by "kissing up" to Big Ed Stash, whom he describes as "a professional assassin who was the Capone mob's top executioner." Alinsky described befriending Stash by listening to Stash talk about women, a conversation many others avoided. Alinsky said within two years he learned from the mob how to hone his skills at organizing for outcomes, saying, "I learned a hell of a lot about the uses and abuses of power from the mob, lessons that stood me in good stead later on, when I was organizing."[33]

Alinsky knew that who controls the language also controls politics. By equipping progressives with the tactics and language needed to advance their agendas, he was able to put conservatives on the defensive, often fighting battles in reactive mode.

In his book, Alinsky laid out thirteen "rules" for progressives to use in order to transform society—and which they implemented with devastating effectiveness in the 1960s and beyond to divide and polarize American society. His most critical rule, as we will see, was number 13: "Pick the target, freeze it, personalize it, and polarize it."

Here are Alinsky's 13 Rules:

1. Power is not only what you have, but what the enemy thinks you have.
2. Never go outside the expertise of your people.
3. Whenever possible, go outside the expertise of the enemy.
4. Make the enemy live up to their own book of rules.
5. Ridicule is man's most potent weapon.
6. A good tactic is one your people enjoy.
7. A tactic that drags on too long becomes a drag.
8. Keep the pressure on.

9. The threat is usually more terrifying than the thing itself.
10. The major premise for tactics is the development of operations that will maintain a constant pressure upon the opposition.
11. If you push a negative hard and deep enough, it will break through into its counterside; this is based on the principle that every positive has its negative.
12. The price of a successful attack is a constructive alternative.[34]

And as previously mentioned:

13. Pick the target, freeze it, personalize it, and polarize it.[35]

The open ridicule of conservatives and American society as a whole was launched in the 1960s as the progressive Left started to take over the news media, entertainment, and other areas of public influence. For each of their issues, they would change the narrative from a negative to a positive (in particular with regard to sexual ethics and illegal drug use), while inventing false threats and picking easy-to-exploit targets to shift public opinion to the progressive way of thought.

Alinsky was also adept at using the tactic of making a small group of dissenters seem larger than they were—thus his first "rule": "Power is not only what you have, but what the enemy thinks you have." As he elaborated, "If your organization is small in numbers, then do what Gideon did: conceal the members in the dark but raise a din and clamor that will make the listener believe that your organization numbers many more than it does. . . . if your organization is too tiny even for noise, stink up the place."[36]

Thus, anti-war protestors, radical leftist students, and other progressives were far outnumbered in American society in the 1960s, but by following Alinsky's playbook, they won the attention of the media who made them seem more numerous and their opinions more widespread than in reality.

This same tactic is used today by groups advocating sexual deviancy, unlimited abortion, and so forth. Their modus operandi was born in the 1960s under Alinsky's tutelage. Meanwhile, they often inflate the numbers and finances of the groups that oppose them in order to make everything seem like a David vs. Goliath battle, when often it is the progressive groups that have the millions, and in many cases, billions more dollars at their disposal.

Alinsky's eighth rule, "Keep the pressure on. Never let up," has been used by various progressive groups to eventually wear down Americans on a number of issues and embrace their goals. While people may still voice objections to all of these, progressives count on the desire of Americans to live peaceful lives and not be constantly in combat mode. By never letting up on the pressure, eventually you wear out the opposition.

Alinsky's fourth rule, "Make the enemy live up to its own book of rules," has been used to attack conservatives, and in particular Christians, if they have (unfortunately) been caught in a transgression. Likewise, the media holds conservatives to a different standard than progressives who violate their own principles. While we are all sinners who fall short of the glory of God, progressives have mocked conservatives, for instance, for not living up to every Old Testament law (which Jesus came to fulfill and free us from) to justify their own rebellion against biblical values.

Thus, as we look at what the '60s wrought and the continued impact on our culture today, we will see nearly all Alinsky's rules have been implemented within every institution. By focusing on dividing Americans, his philosophies helped create the paralyzed, distrustful, and paranoid society in which we currently find ourselves.

Two other socialists, Richard Andrew Cloward and his wife Frances Fox Piven, both sociolgists at Columbia University and who cited Alinsky as their inspiration, wrote out a series of strategies in 1966 to create a socialist state. They were as follows:

1. Control healthcare and you control the people.
2. Increase the poverty level as high as possible, poor people are easier to control and will not fight back if you are providing everything for them to live.
3. Increase the debt to an unsustainable level. That way you are able to increase taxes, and this will produce more poverty.
4. Remove people's ability to defend themselves from the government. That way you are able to create a police state.
5. Take control of every aspect of their lives (food, housing, and income).
6. Take control of what people read and listen to—take control of what children learn in school.
7. Remove the belief in God from the government and the schools.
8. Divide the people into the wealthy and the poor. This will cause more discontent and it will be easier to tax the wealthy with the support of the poor.[37]

We have also seen these aspects of this philosophy implemented in the 1960s, with disastrous results:

1. In 1965, as part of the "Great Society" reforms, President Lyndon Johnson was able to enact Medicare, which ballooned government spending, turned healthcare into a political issue, and paved the way for Obamacare in 2010.

2. The Great Society actually made poverty worse by reducing incentives to work, making people dependent upon the government for income, and undermining the family—in particular the African American family. The result has been increased poverty and crime in our nation's inner cities, while simultaneously demonizing those who have worked hard to be successful.

3. The Great Society also led to massive increase in government spending and has been a major contributor to the national debt crisis our nation now faces. In the 1970s, it led to "stagflation" (recession and inflation occurring at the same time), and it took the painful efforts of Federal Reserve Chairman Paul Volker and President Ronald Reagan to bring interest rates and inflation back under control. Unfortunately, because of the ever-expanding entitlement programs created by progressives in the 1960s, government spending continues to grow and get increasingly out of control.

4. One of the great battlegrounds of our culture is public education. Parents are being increasingly shut out from information about what their children are learning at school—teachings often in conflict with the values parents are still trying to instill in their homes. The progressive Left systematically took over school boards in the 1960s and maintained control (in most cases) ever since, all while labeling conservative parents as "extremists." As a result, children have had the full radical political and sexual agenda of the 1960s forced upon them from an early age in their schoolrooms, and the resulting cancel culture, sexual confusion, and sexual promiscuity is engulfing us today.

5. The Supreme Court decisions of the 1960s in *Engel v. Vitale* (outlawing teachers from starting the school

day with a nonsectarian prayer) and *School District of Abington Township v. Schempp* (outlawing the recitation of the Lord's Prayer and Scripture in public school classrooms even when students had the right to opt out), effectively removed God and any moral foundations from our public schools.

6. By creating and exploiting Trojan Horse issues such as "climate change," "fairness," and "equity," progressives have used fairness phrases to cover power grabs restricting, controlling, and eventually eliminating many of the freedoms Americans have enjoyed—such as travel, the ability to enjoy the fruits of one's labor, and the responsibility and authority to direct the upbringing of one's children.

Thanks to the groundwork laid by the progressives at the turn of the twentieth century and their incremental takeover of American institutions, every aspect of culture—from education to entertainment to family to religion—has been completely transformed. In the following chapters, we are going to look at each of those areas and how the radical activists of the 1960s seized control to achieve their agenda of an America that rejects the ideals upon which it was founded.

CHAPTER THREE

The Moral Stumble

Along with philosophies held by Woodrow Wilson, the *Port Huron Statement*, and Saul Alinksy, another main contributor to our current cultural abyss is the radical sexual revolution of the 1960s. This revolution was ushered in through the work of Dr. Alfred Kinsey, along with the writings of other progressive academics, such as the previously mentioned Herbert Marcuse and Sigmund Freud.

To go into all the philosophies that contributed to the sexual revolution would be another book entirely, and has already been written by Carl Trueman. It is titled, *Strange New World*, and chronicles in great detail the role each of these individuals held in creating a culture based on pleasure of self.

However, for the purpose of this book, I am going to look at the main contributors in the decades directly preceding the 1960s, all of whom were disciples of the individuals I have mentioned above.

In 1948, Dr. Kinsey produced *Sexual Behavior in the Human Male*, funded by the Rockefeller Foundation, using dubious research methods at best, to set the stage for the sexual revolution of the 1960s and all the social pathologies that came with it. It, along with his 1953 report, *Sexual*

Behavior in the Human Female, became collectively known as the Kinsey Report.

Kinsey died in 1956, but not before he established the cornerstone for modern sex education and reshaped American's attitudes toward sex, especially with regard to what was seen to be aberrant sexual behavior at the time. It was Kinsey who normalized these behaviors, elevating aberrance while mocking normal human sexuality.

The 1990 book *Kinsey, Sex and Fraud* exposed the fraudulence of Kinsey's research. Kinsey's male sample was skewed to provide much higher numbers of sexual deviancy than was common in the general public.

For instance, 25 percent of the men in his sample were prisoners and ex-cons, with an abnormal percentage being sex offenders. Others reported participating in sex lectures which they'd attended to get help with sexual problems. Finally, many of the others surveyed were underworld figures and leaders of groups outside the mainstream of human sexuality, including at least 200 male prostitutes.

What segments of society were underrepresented in Kinsey's sample? The marginalized segments included churchgoers, married couples, and those with higher educational levels—basically the majority of Americans at the time.[1]

In his biography of Kinsey, author James H. Jones wrote that Kinsey would allow "research subjects" to engage in child sexual abuse. In addition, he would film his employees and subordinates engaging in sexual activity, enter rooms while his naked students were showering, engage in sex with his "research subjects," and write obscene letters to his assistants.[2]

But Kinsey had his critics, even among liberal academia, such as anthropologists Margaret Mead and Ruth Benedict; Stanford University psychologist Lewis M. Terman; Karl Menninger, M.D. (founder of the famed Menninger

Institute); psychiatrists Eric Fromm and Lawrence Kubie; and cultural critic Lionel Trilling of Columbia University.[3] Kinsey's skewed research claimed greatly inflated percentages of people engaging in same-sex behavior (It was Kinsey who first came up with the statistic that 10 percent of the American population is homosexual)[4] as well as higher percentages of couples engaging in premarital sex. These claims led or at least enabled, the academic community and entertainment industry to openly question and mock long-held American sexual mores—a significant cultural phenomenon we'll examine in greater depth later in this book.

Investigative journalist Sue Ellin Browder writes:

> Many traditionally forbidden sexual practices, Kinsey and his colleagues proclaimed, were surprisingly commonplace; 85 percent of men and 48 percent of women said they'd had premarital sex, and 50 percent of men and 40 percent of women had been unfaithful after marriage. Incredibly, 71 percent of women claimed their affair hadn't hurt their marriage, and a few even said it had helped. What's more, 69 percent of men had been with prostitutes, 10 percent had been homosexual for at least three years, and 17 percent of farm boys had experienced sex with animals. Implicit in Kinsey's report was the notion that these behaviors were biologically "normal" and hurt no one. Therefore, people should act on their impulses with no inhibition or guilt.[5]

To quote Carl Trueman, "In short, the tradition of seeing the world as driven by sex that Kinsey's reports inaugurate is responsible for the fact that we now see the world as driven by sex."[6]

The Kinsey Report not only ignited the sexual revolution of the 1960s, but it also made "victims" out of those who had been "sexually repressed." As Anne Hendershott writes in her book *The Politics of Deviance*, "In the aftermath of the radical egalitarianism of the 1960s, merely to label a behavior as deviant came to be viewed as rejecting the equality—perhaps the humanity—of those engaging in it."[7] The tables were turned, and society would eventually label those who believed in heterosexual marriage and monogamy as "deviant" and the "deviant" behaviors as normal.

Thus, Kinsey's "victims"—the "sexually repressed" capitalized on the societal change of the 1960s to not only excuse, but ultimately, exalt their behavior. As Hendershott states:

> Nobody was stamped as deviant—except, of course, those unfortunate traditionalists whom the new power elite in academia and in the media increasingly saw as maintaining an outworn and always suspect middle-class ideology about deviance.[8]

It was Kinsey's work that inspired Hugh Hefner, whom I will discuss later, to create *Playboy* magazine. It also encouraged Helen Gurley Brown to turn *Cosmopolitan* magazine into a sex manual for women. Kinsey took the pornography industry, which was mostly underground, and made it mainstream—resulting in millions of broken lives and marriages.

Following on Kinsey's heels came William H. Masters and Virginia E. Johnson, better known simply as "Masters and Johnson." Starting in 1957, they researched human sexual response, along with the diagnosis and treatment of various sexual disorders and dysfunctions.

Like Kinsey, their work ushered in the sexual revolution of the 1960s through their frank discussions of human sexuality, promotion of premarital and extramarital sex, and advocacy of other forms of deviant sexual behavior.

Masters and Johnson first met in 1957 when Johnson was hired by Masters to serve as a research assistant for a comprehensive study he wanted to do on human sexuality. They hooked wires to paid volunteers engaging in sexual activity to monitor response, and Masters and Johnson also joined in, having sexual intercourse with each other and eventually entering into, for Masters who was married, an adulterous relationship.

While Kinsey used the "sexually repressed" among his research "sample," Masters and Johnson used prostitutes because, in their view, they were "socially isolated," regularly engaged in sex, and had no problem cooperating. Again, not ordinary Americans.

Eventually they moved on from prostitutes and recruited 382 women and 312 men from their community to participate—with the majority being white, highly educated, and married.[9] Monogamy was quickly thrown out the window as men and women were randomly paired to become "assigned couples."

I will not go into graphic detail about their research, which also included male and female homosexual couples, whom they tried to convert to heterosexuality. The key takeaway is their sex research was trumpeted throughout the media and played a role in ushering in the destructive sexual revolution, including activities such as "swinging" (couples engaging in sexual behavior with each other's respective spouses) and so forth.

The work of Kinsey and Masters and Johnson convinced many Americans that monogamy was boring, ultimately encouraging pornography usage and assaults on marriage such as polyamory. It also provided dubious research to back up claims that Americans were far more sexually active than they really are—and encouraged people to "unleash" their so-called sexual inhibitions and experiment with a multitude of sexual behaviors.

And in the 1960s, they were unleashed.

At its core, this sexual revolution replaced the self-sacrifice required of both spouses to make a marriage work with a selfish "all about me" philosophy based on personal "satisfaction" rather than mutual respect. Once it became all about sex, love and commitment took a back seat.

Throw in "the pill," which I will discuss next, and this toxic combination of sexual propaganda paved the way for so many of our social dysfunctions—divorce, out-of-wedlock pregnancies, cohabitation, gender confusion, rampant infidelity, and ultimately the breakdown of the family, and with it, lost generations of children left to fend themselves with either just one parent, or no parents at all.

"THE PILL"

In his book, *The Fractured Republic,* Yuval Levin writes:

> Ultimately, the sexual revolution ... was surely the most culturally transformative of all the waves of change, liberation, and individualism that swept over American life in the postwar era and in one way or another it was connected to all the others. In a time of rapid technological process in many arenas, no technology was as transformative as the birth control pill. [10]

With the advent and legalization of the birth control pill in the mid-1960s, procreation could now be detached from sexual activity, and thus serve as the launching pad for the fires of sexual revolution stoked by Kinsey and Masters and Johnson.

Carl Trueman writes:

> [The advent of the pill] allowed women to take control of their own fertility and made it very easy to sever the link between sex and pregnancy. This changed the

context of sexual activity. . . . With the pill, the risks (financial and social) of sex were dramatically lowered. The idea of sex as a pleasant recreation without the need for a long-term commitment is simply far more plausible in a world with access to the pill.[11]

Four people played a critical role in the creation of the pill. The first, and perhaps most recognized, was Margaret Sanger who founded Planned Parenthood, and as a eugenicist and friend of Roger Baldwin (founder of the ACLU), she believed in the termination of those she deemed to be "inferiors." Three lesser-known contributors were scientist Gregory Pinkus, who experimented with in-vitro fertilization, a Catholic obstetrician named John Rock, and an elderly heiress, Katharine McCormick, who provided the funding for the research.

Former *Wall Street Journal* reporter Jonathan Eig noted these four individuals engaged in a lot of subterfuge to hide what they were up to. This has been a modus operandi of progressives on nearly every issue—to deny or lie about their actions or intentions to lull the public to sleep while quietly implementing their agenda behind the scenes. Eig writes:

> There's a lot of lying in this process of creating the first oral contraceptive. That's what they have to do. You can really have a wonderful ethical discussion and debate about whether it was worth it, whether they were doing things that were beyond the bounds. The laws and the ethics of science were very different in the 1950s than they are today — you didn't have to give informed consent, you didn't have to have anybody sign forms giving away their rights, telling them about what these experiments are for. So, in a way, we do have women being treated like lab animals so that we may find a form of birth control that frees them. There's a great irony there.[12]

The pill would also transform the relationship between men and women, in most cases, in a negative manner for women.

Eig concludes:

> I was listening to a rabbi's sermon — this was maybe five or six years ago — and he began by saying that the birth control pill may have been the most important invention of the 20th century. My immediate reaction was, 'That's nuts. That can't possibly be. I can think of six things off the top of my head that seemed more important than that.' But it stayed with me. I kept thinking about it. A couple of years went by, and I was still thinking about it. His case was that it had changed more than just science, more than just medicine. It had changed human dynamics. It had changed the way men and women get along in the world. It changed reproduction, obviously, but it also created all kinds of opportunities for women that weren't there before, it had spread democracy.[13]

But while some celebrated the new opportunities available for women, there were many negative ramifications for women and society as well.

My colleague at Focus on the Family, Glenn Stanton, interviewed Professor Bruce Wydick, an economist at the University of San Francisco, who specializes in family relationships. Wydick said, "A world where social norms dictate that sex and commitment go together is a world that upholds the happiness and dignity of women. . . . The revolution that brought sexual freedom allowed women to unwittingly undercut each other in the competition for men, providing men greater access to more sex for lower and lower levels of commitment, to the obvious benefit of the men."

He concluded, "Women's sexual freedom became the greatest thing that ever happened to men who wanted as much sex as possible with as little commitment as possible, and hence made women much worse off."[14]

Some feminists recognize this. Alice Schwarzer said, "Before [the pill] came along, young girls and women simply got married. And now? With the pill, things were turned upside down and women had to be up for it. If a woman wasn't taking the pill, people would start saying, 'she's too narrow-minded, and nobody had danced with her so far.' Women were permanently at men's sexual disposal. And men took no responsibility for any consequences that might arise."[15]

The pill took away the need for men to grow up and take responsibility as a husband and father because their sexual urges could be met without ever making any real commitment.

All these factors—Kinsey, Masters and Johnson, the pill, etc.—laid the groundwork for the sexual revolution of the 1960s. It did not just happen overnight. The social earthquake of the 1960s was created by all these individuals who came before—paving the way for those who moved forward to implement these agendas.

Chapters 2 and 3 painted the big-picture reasons how the 1960s led us to where we are today. My hope is that I can provide a roadmap for how we can turn America around before it is too late. But we must understand the past before we can understand the present and change the future. We will start with looking at how progressives took over American education.

CHAPTER FOUR

The Education Stumble

To understand the NEA—to understand the union—
read Saul Alinsky. If you read Rules for Radicals, you
will understand the NEA more profoundly than reading
anything else. Because the whole organization was mod-
eled on that kind of behavior which was really begun when
the NEA used Saul Alinsky as a consultant to train their
own staff.[1]

—Former National Education Association
Leader John Lloyd

One of my good friends lives in a quiet neighborhood near a public high school in suburban Phoenix, Arizona. Because he works remotely, he often sees the teenagers attending there either walk home or be picked up by family or friends every afternoon.

As he watches the young people leave school, he cannot help but note the blank expressions on their faces. There is no joy, no enthusiasm, only a zombie-like stare or a head buried in a smartphone. It quickly becomes evident that instead of spending a day enjoying the opportunity to learn and grow, they have just endured another day in an educational system providing no hope and little, if any, practical skills needed to succeed in life.

My friend also observes the parents who come to pick up these students every day at about 2:00 p.m. These parents are probably sitting in their cars, hoping their children are learning the life and critical thinking skills they need to succeed. But he knows, much to their dismay, their children are probably not. Then, every May, he sees these same parents arrive at their children's graduation ceremonies to celebrate their children's achievement of surviving the public education system with the hope the diploma they receive will be the first step in a successful launch into adulthood.

Unfortunately, it won't, as many employers find out when these young men and women enter the workforce with practically no ability to perform or hold a job where basic language and math skills are essential.

At the same time, these parents are perceived by the educational establishment as serving no greater purpose than creating these children so they can be handed over to a system that will indoctrinate them with the proper worldview. As one Florida school teacher said, these parents have "no rights" once they drop their children off at the schoolhouse door.[2] That includes, in some cases, if their male child chooses to be a female and vice versa.

While my friend's observations are anecdotal, his conclusions are backed by the dismal test scores produced from our public education system, particularly when it comes to civic education.

A 2018 survey conducted by the Woodrow Wilson National Fellowship Foundation investigating the civic and historical knowledge of people in all fifty states found only 53 percent were able to earn a passing grade in U.S. history. Eighty-five percent could not identify the year the U.S. Constitution was written. Even more alarmingly, one in four people did not know freedom of speech was guaranteed under the Constitution.[3]

Ignorance is not confined to civics—it extends to American history as well. Seventy-two percent of those surveyed did not know which states comprised the original thirteen colonies; 37 percent believed Benjamin Franklin invented the light bulb; only 24 percent knew colonists fought the Revolutionary War over unjust taxation; and 12 percent believed Dwight Eisenhower led the military in the American Civil War (thirty years before he was born!). Finally, while most managed to identify the cause of the Cold War, two percent said climate change caused the Cold War![4]

Here are some more sobering statistics:

- According to ProLiteracy, more than 30 million adults in the United States cannot read, write, or do basic math above a third-grade level.[5]
- The National Bureau of Economic Research states that children whose parents have low literacy rates have a 72 percent change of being at the lowest reading levels themselves—resulting in poor grades, displaying behavioral problems, repeating grades, and even dropping out of school.[6]
- The *American Journal of Public Health* indicates that low literacy is connected to more than $230 billion in health care costs annually, as almost half of Americans cannot read well enough to understand basic health information, and thus incur greater costs.[7]

If you are going to attack America's foundations, the place to start, as all demagogues and dictators have discovered, is with the youth. The young are malleable and easy to influence because their minds have yet to develop the critical thinking skills needed to discern truth from error. They are often emotionally, rather than intellectually, driven and thus ripe for conversion to progressive causes.

Every totalitarian regime, from the Soviet Union to Nazi Germany has focused on recruiting the youth to achieve their aims. And as the 1960s showed, it was America's youth, who carried the water for progressives set on advancing their own agenda.

And if you provide them with an inadequate education, all the easier to manipulate them to do what you wish.

It is for that exact reason progressives, starting with John Dewey, a self-proclaimed humanist and "democratic socialist," created our current public education system. Dewey wrote in 1904 how public education would bring about a "new social order."[8] Since Dewey rejected Christianity and the existence of God, Dewey's new social order rejected moral absolutes and focused on creating a new collective morality to replace biblical morality.

To quote Henry T. Edmonson III, professor of political science at Georgia College, "A sound understanding of the philosophical underpinnings of American education is impossible without a firm grasp of John Dewey's contribution. Although the ideas of Thomas Jefferson, George Washington, Dr. Benjamin Rush, and others of the founding generation still enjoy moderate influence here and there in American schools and universities, the prestige of Dewey's thought has long superseded that of the founders."[9]

Dewey and his followers saw education as a sociological tool for shaping individuals to fit into society in a certain way. In his utopian vision, as outlined in his 1933 speech to the Teachers College at Columbia University, Dewey said learning should be de-emphasized and replaced with the creation of attitudes as a way of accomplishing social change.[10]

Harry T. Edmonson III comments, "Dewey's thought is characterized by hostility, not only to traditional religion, but to all abstract and metaphysical ideas. . . . He argues, for example, that belief in objective truth and authoritative notions of good and evil are harmful to students."[11]

Religion, in Dewey's view, had "lost itself in cults, dogmas, and myths," and he believed like the German philosopher Friedrich Nietzsche, it created a "slave mentality" resulting in "an intolerant superiority on the part of the few and an intolerable burden on the part of the many."[12] Edmonson adds, "Dewey's unrelenting attack on religion and traditional education is a conspicuous feature of his educational philosophy. . . . Dewey makes little attempt to veil his hostility to Christianity in particular."[13]

Dewey wrote, "For Christendom as a whole, morality has been connected with supernatural commands, rewards, and penalties." He goes on to call Christianity a "dying myth" and states he is proud of those who have "escaped this delusion."[14] He states that religion "has made morals fanatic or fantastic, sentimental or authoritative by severing them from actual facts and forces."[15] At a celebration of his 90th birthday, Dewey said education can only be effective if individuals "are progressively liberated from bondage to prejudice and ignorance," i.e., orthodox faith.[16]

Given these prejudices, it was only natural for Dewey to reject the very principles and God-given rights our nation was founded on, such as the right to life, property, and free markets. He also wrote in 1935, "Organized social planning is now the sole method of social action by which liberalism can realize its professed aims."[17] In his earlier 1916 work, *Democracy and Education*, Dewey stated, the education regime he hoped to implement would be "the process through which the needed transformation may be accomplished."[18]

Edmonson concludes, "To the extent American education has absorbed Dewey's enmity against religion, students and parents legitimately question whether their own values receive due respect in our liberal pluralistic society. Nowhere has genuine faith been more scorned, both by condescension and hostility, than in the halls of the educational establishment."[19]

In the first chapter, I mentioned the Supreme Court decisions striking down teacher-led nonsectarian prayer, the reading of Scripture, and reciting the Lord's Prayer in public schools. It is no coincidence that many of the major religious liberty court cases over the past hundred years have involved public education—from school prayer to graduation invocations to equal access for Christian clubs to school facilities.

The first case was *Engel v. Vitale* (1962) in which the Supreme Court held public school teachers could not open a class with a prayer, even if the prayer was nonsectarian and the schools did not compel a student to join in prayer over their or their parents' objection.[20]

Engel was followed the next year (1963) by *School District of Abington Township v. Schempp*, which held the state could not require the recitation of the Lord's Prayer or the reading of Scripture in public school classrooms, even if students had the right to opt out from these activities.[21]

While unruly behavior in public schools has always been a problem at one level or another, the tradition of voluntary prayer helped provide some sort of moral compass and discipline, even for the worst bullies and disrupters. It provided an expected standard for acceptable, and non-acceptable, behavior, as well as respect for authority.

Without such a standard, classrooms quickly descended into chaos. Without defined rules based on the commonly held cultural and religious standards of the Ten Commandments to guide them, all of a sudden any and every type of behavior was excused, and in some cases, accepted.

The result was not only unsafe schools, but ever-decreasing test scores, as it becomes nearly impossible to teach or learn anything when a school day is filled more with disciplinary disruptions than actual classroom learning.

Besides the removal of God from the public schools, other factors from the 1960s took a wrecking ball to our public education system. The breakdown of the family, which I will discuss in a forthcoming chapter, resulted in increasing numbers of children coming to school with not only behavioral issues, but emotional ones as well. As mentioned earlier, progressive activists also saw public education as a venue to treat children more like test animals to experiment upon rather than actual human beings. New teaching methods for math, reading, and writing were introduced—discarding those that worked quite well for the first half of the twentieth century. Second, social activism was stressed because young minds are much easier to mold than older ones because they are still in the process of being "hard-wired" and susceptible to emotionally based arguments.

Thus, as the letter in chapter 1 from the pen pal said, his school suddenly went from singing "My Country 'Tis of Thee" to "If I Had a Hammer" with nary a thought.

Thus, right from the beginning with Dewey's work, public education became a progressive tool to achieve cultural transformation and hostility to faith. However, until the 1960s, common cultural understanding kept it from veering drastically hard left. In the 1960s, however, with that cultural consensus gone, public education became increasingly less about education and increasingly more about indoctrination.

While it took several decades to fulfill John Dewey's vision, as hatched in the early part of the twentieth century, it finally came to fruition in the 1960s, and our educational system has never been the same since.

DEWEY'S UTOPIAN VISION

Like other progressives such as the ACLU's Roger Baldwin, Dewey visited the Soviet Union in the 1920s and brought back glowing reports about the Soviet Union's "collective" form of education and society,[22] while conveniently ignoring or oblivious to the millions being slaughtered to create such a society.

Dewey, thus, created an educational system no longer parent-driven, but driven and controlled by the state to create cultural, political, and philosophical uniformity. Parents, in many ways, were reduced to mere breeders, existing merely to turn their children over to the state for indoctrination and reprogramming to reject the views of their parents and instead embrace the "collective thought" of progressives—collective thought purposely excluding all viewpoints except those approved by the state. Dewey's thinking epitomizes America's public education system today.

Dewey made his thoughts clear when he wrote in 1898 that the educational system should no longer emphasize reading, writing, and arithmetic during the early part of a child's education, but instead should focus on socialization and collectivism. He also recognized, as many other progressives like Roger Baldwin did, this transformation would require time and must be made incrementally so people would accept gradual changes without becoming alarmed or even particularly noticing what was happening. Dewey wrote, "Change must come naturally. To force it unduly would compromise its final success by favoring a violent reaction."[23]

To that end, Dewey did what so many progressives did and continue to do to this day—find a wealthy benefactor to fund his "vision." In Dewey's case, that benefactor was John D. Rockefeller, the possessor of the Standard Oil fortune (As mentioned earlier, the Rockefeller Foundation also funded the work of Alfred Kinsey). Dewey accepted a job at the University of Chicago, which coincidentally was also supported financially by Rockefeller, and then moved on to Columbia University's Teachers College. With these positions, he had the academic legitimacy to implement his collective vision.

And that vision has resulted in the end of education in America—with children graduating high school with little to no marketable skills, a general inability to manage their own affairs, but thoroughly indoctrinated to scream about rights while avoiding responsibility.

Even some progressives are seeing this. The leftist Center for American Progress has concluded our present educational system turns out "a large percentage of students [who] land a high school diploma that is basically meaningless. The document might indicate that the students are ready for college, but in reality, the students simply do not have the necessary skills or knowledge."[24] That statement is sad but has been increasingly true.

The failure of our educational system, which at one time was the envy of the developed world, started to occur in the 1960s as academics, now fully trained in Dewey's utopian vision (as outlined in the *Port Huron Statement*), moved into influential positions as school administrators and school board members. These same academics also began training a new generation of teachers to be more focused on political agendas and using children as guinea pigs to test out new experimental learning theories, often without the consent or knowledge of their parents. Critical race theory and gender identity theory are just the latest radical manifestations.

As called for by the *Port Huron Statement*, teachers' unions were radicalized through a leftist takeover of all key leadership positions. Thus, we now have teachers' unions advocating for radical social issues, such as unrestricted access to abortion, transgender rights, and of course, ever-increasing government funding to push their agendas in the classroom. And again, this radicalization of teachers' unions brought them into alignment with the beliefs of John Dewey.

This progressive dismantling of the American system for educating children with the basic skills needed to survive in life has been completed with devastating results, and our society is paying the price.

EXPERIMENTING WITH CHILDREN'S LIVES

One of the great losses from our educational system, as ushered in during the 1960s, is the removal of teaching critical thinking skills. Up until the 1960s, despite the utopian dreams of Dewey and other progressives, children were taught how to think about and debate issues. This enabled them to become morally mature individuals who were equipped with the intellectual tools to make sound judgments about morally complex situations and to separate fact from fiction. While not every child received an "A" or "B" in critical thinking skills, at least they were taught the basics and the concept of critical thinking was valued.

Then came the 1960s. Critical thinking skills became seen as "judgmental" or as encouraging "oppression." It is no wonder we now have the chaos we do because without critical thinking skills, people are inclined to follow the natural human tendency to make decisions based solely on their emotions, and without reference to (or sometimes even acknowledgment of) facts.

Our current national problems with so-called "fake news" can be directly traced to tossing out critical thinking in the 1960s through our educational system. With no understanding of history or civics, and no ability to discern truth from error, we have become a nation, like Pavlov's dog, which salivates every time a bell is rung with the latest misinformation.

Another "transformation" occurred in the 1960s in the teaching of math, and it left an entire generation not only unable to do basic arithmetic, but also frightened to even tackle the subject. One observer of the effect "new math" had on students (as well as parents and teachers) is Karen Harris. She writes:

> There are two words that still scare teachers and schoolchildren of the 1960s: New Math. This dreaded and traumatic change in the teaching of basic mathematics had young kids pondering abstract algebra, modular arithmetic, matrices, symbolic logic, Boolean algebra, and other super-mathy stuff they might never need. New Math confused everybody and didn't seem to pay off—kids were wrangling with abstract ideas about math without actually being able to get the right answer.
>
> Much of the concept of New Math was retraining the brain to think of math in abstract ways. The theoretical components were blended in with the concrete math and a new, intimidating vocabulary was introduced that included terms like "Boolean algebra" and "Matrices." Students who were still learning their multiplication tables were being taught to find the value of "x." They had to understand the difference between numbers and numerals, as well as symbolic logic. Students were learning about things like "truth sets" and "commutative law," but not learning simple arithmetic.[25]

New math was the invention of ivory tower academics who tried to introduce complex theoretical concepts into minds still trying to figure out 2+2 and 3×3. A famous *Peanuts* cartoon, by the late Charles Schulz, summed up what young children were facing on a daily basis as they were used like lab animals to test out this "New Math" teaching method.

Sally is reading a test question out loud: "Renaming Two . . . Subsets . . . Joining Sets . . . Number Sentences . . . Placeholders . . ." Finally, in total frustration, she screams,

"ALL I WANT TO KNOW IS, HOW MUCH IS TWO AND TWO?"

Eventually, like so many ill-conceived reforms, "New Math" was rejected and tossed out of public schools, but not before an entire generation of students came to loathe the subject and had no idea how to do even the most basic of mathematical equations.

The other "reform" that set our educational system going down the wrong track in the 1960s was the federal takeover of education via the so-called "Great Society" reforms—which I will discuss throughout this book. Major federal intervention into local schools began with the Elementary and Secondary Education Act of 1965 (ESEA). This took authority away from local school boards to develop curriculum that fit best for their communities and sent America down the road toward a national "one-size-fits-all" approach that fit no one.

For instance, a student in rural Iowa needs to learn a different skill set to thrive in his community than a student in downtown New York City. But by not taking this into consideration, the educational system fails them both.

This "reform" is in alignment with the goals of the *Port Huron Statement*, which basically called for the "re-education" of rural America so their views and values would be in alignment with progressive urbanites. By nationalizing education (and in their view someday "internationalizing" it), progressives could, at first stealthily, reshape the minds of young children in areas they could not previously reach, and by teaching them to reject their parents' values turn this next generation of children into foot soldiers for the progressive agenda.

And of course, as with any government program, a massive bureaucracy was created, which is why in the 1960s begins the trend of the ratio of administrators to teachers greatly increasing. With more edicts and interference in the classroom and more education funds going to the administrators responsible, our children quickly became the ones who lost the most, with test scores declining nearly every year.

From 1965–1980, the SAT—the test taken by seniors for college admission—verbal score dropped from 478 in 1963 to 424 in 1980. The SAT mathematics score declined from 502 in 1963 to 465 in 1980.[26] Federal involvement in education in the 1960s was supposed to help poor students receive a better education—instead they have received a *worse* one—and thus the gap between poor and rich has only grown larger.

However, I would suggest perhaps this was the goal anyway. Without critical thinking skills and competency in basic life skills, people are more easily swayed toward radical positions, leading to more people dependent upon government to take care of their basic needs.

Therefore, so much of our current educational nightmare is the result of the radicalization of public education in the 1960s, whether it be through the pushing of progressive agendas in the classroom, the turning of children into guinea pigs to test unproven learning theories, or the creation of national one-size-fits-all teaching standards that deny the uniqueness of the individual and the community in which they live.

It is also the result of parents being pushed aside by educators who believe they know best. This arrogance, which many Americans are thankfully beginning to wake up to, emerged in the 1960s. If we are going to regain control of our nation's educational system, parents must no longer stay in denial about what occurs once the classroom door is shut, because while we may think, "that's not going on at my child's school," it surely is. And unless we reverse the educational bankruptcy started in the 1960s, our nation will continue in a downward spiral—economically, competitively, and spiritually.

CHAPTER FIVE

The Entertainment Stumble

In the war for the American mind, entertainment pro-grams have become political territory.[1]
—Kathryn Montgomery

The sexual revolution, whose attitudes, diffused through-out culture by advertising, movies, popular movies, and television, so transformed values and behavior that they ultimately reshaped family life, increasing divorce, illegiti-macy, and female-headed families on all levels of society.[2]
—Myron Magnet

In the 1950s, television largely mirrored the prevalent concept of the American family. Popular shows like "Leave it to Beaver" and "Father Knows Best" depicted the fam-ily as a heterosexual, patriarchal, churchgoing unit with chaste children. But in the 1960s, family depictions began to change. And so did America's thinking.[3]
—Jonathan Merritt

CBS canceled everything with a tree in it— includ-ing Lassie.[4]
—Pat Buttram

The 1960s also brought the radicalization of American entertainment. The Production Code, which limited depictions of sex and violence on screen was cast aside, and Hollywood quickly adopted an "anything goes" approach with films depicting nudity, explicit sexuality, and graphic violence.

In the theatre world, *Hair* promoted the "counterculture" with its plea for "harmony and understanding" including disrespect for the American flag, widespread profanity, celebration of illegal drug use, and nudity. The days of *My Fair Lady* and *The Sound of Music* faded away for this brave new world of entertainment.[5]

Meanwhile, television programs went from presenting the family as a cultural ideal, as in shows like *The Andy Griffith Show* and *The Adventures of Ozzie and Harriet*, to a relic to be ridiculed and redefined. Entertainment was transformed—seemingly in a blink of an eye—from something that brought people together into another method to divide society and pit Americans against each other, as well as an avenue to slowly indoctrinate them to accept progressive beliefs.

The result has been a coarsening of society and the glorification of dangerous behaviors, particularly to children and teenagers—the most vulnerable members of our society.

To do an extensive look at how the entertainment industry has negatively impacted American culture over the past sixty years would require an entire book. So I am choosing to focus on the key individuals who helped turn the American entertainment industry from celebrating American values of faith, responsibility, and sacrifice to mocking and belittling those values.

NORMAN LEAR AND *ALL IN THE FAMILY*

The chief architect of this coarsening via network television in the late 1960s and early 1970s was the late Norman Lear who passed away in December 2023 at the age of 101. As Al Mohler writes, "[Lear] ranks among the most significant forces of moral change in modern times. He might well have been the most influential liberal figure in American life at a time when the country was turning left, hard left, on many moral issues. . . . He wanted to change America, and he did."[6] In fact, upon the news of Lear's death, many articles trumpeted how he had accomplished his mission of cultural change. Of course, they did so in glowing terms, instead of examining the dark and cynical path he placed our country and culture on.

For many, the situational comedies, or sitcoms, airing in the early to mid-1960s are still a joy to watch today. There is a great bit of nostalgia and happy memories associated with programs such as *Leave It to Beaver*, *The Beverly Hillbillies*, *Petticoat Junction*, *The Andy Griffith Show*, *Hogan's Heroes*, *The Dick Van Dyke Show*, and others. And if you desired something beyond comedy, there were solid, character-driven shows such as *Perry Mason* and *Mission: Impossible*. In fact, many attorneys cite *Perry Mason* as the reason they chose to become an attorney. These shows continue to be watched and loved via streaming platforms or DVD to this day.

Regardless the personal politics of those involved in creating these shows (most of them were admittedly liberal—particularly on *The Dick Van Dyke Show*), there was no overt political agenda in play. Any political statements were made subtly, instead of with a hammer to the head, as would start to occur as the 1960s wore on.

Shows were mostly apolitical and sought to affirm basic American ideals: good over evil, hard work, personal sacrifice, and treating others with dignity and respect, regardless of their personal quirks (a recurring theme in many of the comedies of the era). The most shocking items were Mary Tyler Moore wearing capri pants on *The Dick Van Dyke Show* instead of the dresses and pearl necklaces worn by

Barbara Billingsley on *Leave It to Beaver*, or the implied "skinny-dipping" by the Bradley sisters in the water tower on *Petticoat Junction*.

Then the great purge of many of these highly-rated family-oriented programs occurred—starting in the late 1960s and culminating in the early 1970s. In place of these classic shows came a flood of new content filled with cynicism, the glorification of evil, and the mocking of others.

The creators of these new shows knew about television's ability to change culture. As Kathryn Montgomery writes, ". . . television's greatest power is in its role as the central storyteller for the culture. It is the fiction programming, more than news and public affairs, that most effectively embodies and reinforces the dominant values in American society. This is what has made television such a critical target for political groups."[7]

In the current cultural battle between rural America and its values and urban America, the first shot was fired in what was to be called the "rural purge" of television stemming out of the 1960s. Like the "cancel culture" of today, all these successful shows had to be eliminated by new ones pushing a progressive agenda. As a result, our society became coarser and divided.

As one commentor has stated, "Although they admitted in private notes to each other that 'ratings indicate that the American public prefers hillbillies, cowboys, and spies,' the eager new programming executives wanted new shows and characters that reflected *themselves*: elite, wealthy, urban, ambitious, university-educated, progressive and sexually liberated. Especially sexually liberated. A new phrase appeared: 'Pushing the envelope.'"[8]

In the case of comedy, the person pushing the envelope was Norman Lear. But he not only pushed it, he also opened it and unleashed cultural venom impacting our society to this day.

Lear started laying the foundation for his cultural hijacking of American entertainment in the late 1960s. In 1967, he released a movie, *Divorce American Style*, with the before-mentioned Dick Van Dyke along with Debbie Reynolds, which openly mocked the institution of marriage. Lear then turned his sights on attacking other cultural institutions via network television, which brought his agenda directly into American homes for tens of millions of people.

In the words of Al Mohler, "How did Lear drive American morality to the Left? He did so by creating stories that made America laugh—and sometimes cringe. . . . Driven by his liberal passions and a determination to force political change through television, Lear built a progressivist empire, eventually championing causes that ranged from abortion to sexual liberation, feminism, and the welfare state. . . . We are all living in Norman Lear's world now."[9]

Lear's first hit, *All in the Family*, debuted in 1971. In an early episode, Archie, the conservative, bigoted straw man Lear created to mock, finds out one of his buddies at the bar, a perceived "man's man," is gay. Lear would eventually introduce a cross-dressing character, whose death results in Archie's wife Edith questioning her faith. Edith would also discover she had a lesbian cousin. Lear also included stories on male impotence, menopause, and other formerly taboo topics on the show.

In fact, the first episode of *All in the Family* began with a disclaimer: "The program you are about to see is *All in the Family*. It seeks to throw a humorous spotlight on our frailties, prejudices, and concerns. By making them a source of laughter, we hope to show—in a mature fashion—just how absurd they are."[10]

Thus, Lear was upfront about his intentions, saying he deliberately portrayed the character of Archie Bunker as a "poorly educated, full-of-himself blowhard . . . spewing a kind of rancid, lights-out conservatism."[11]

All in the Family was a hit and quickly led to Lear's second show, *Maude*, about Archie's progressive cousin who Lear said was probably closest to him in terms of worldview.[12] *Maude* included a story about the title character choosing to have an abortion[13] which aired just prior to the *Roe v. Wade* decision. Maude and her family also repeatedly mocked the patriotism and moral values of Maude's conservative neighbor.

Progressive elites were exhilarated as they saw network television not only embracing but advancing their agenda of mocking the faith and values of everyday Americans. Progressives recognized, very astutely, the use of humor would greatly advance their goals. Humor has a tremendous power to soften people up to gradually accept new ideas—in this case, progressive ideals. In many ways, mocking ideas is a form of cultural grooming to get someone to agree with you by weakening their resistance.

This is something Lear knew, as he wrote, "Comedy with something serious in mind works as an intravenous to the mind and spirit."[14]

In 1999 President Bill Clinton honored Lear with the National Medal of Arts, proclaiming he "held up a mirror to American society and changed the way we look at it."[15] That statement was sadly true. Lear changed the way we looked at American society—for the worse. He took our sunny optimism and national unity and turned them into a dark cloud of cynicism and division.

Probably the most telling comment made by Lear about his views on faith and patriotism was made in a July 2002 PBS interview with Bill Moyers. Moyers asked him, "Did your heart leap with joy last week when the Federal Court in California said that the Pledge of Allegiance is unconstitutional because that phrase 'one nation, Under God' violates the separation of church and state?" Lear replied: "I won't say that I was pleased; [but] I wasn't upset."[16]

Lear also founded People for the American Way, an organization dedicated to advancing his progressive agenda while demonizing religious conservatives, and he produced and aired a television special titled "I Love Liberty," with a who's-who of entertainment leftists such as Jane Fonda and Barbra Streisand, which served basically as a fundraiser for his organization.[17]

All in the Family and *Maude* begot shows by other producers, but which also pushed progressive themes, such as *M*A*S*H,* which openly mocked faith, the military, and America's role in the world (which was often portrayed as villainous or clueless). The only faith allowed was one that was "inclusive" and did not have moral absolutes. Progressives were on a roll, and by the mid-seventies, the shows exemplifying the values of the majority of Americans had virtually disappeared from the television landscape, replaced by progressive sermons in half-hour and hour-long formats. As Pat Buttram, who portrayed the con man Mr. Haney on *Green Acres* noted, every show with a tree had been cancelled. In place of trees, Lear and his allies planted weeds choking off the American spirit.

THE NEW HOLLYWOOD

Television though was merely following culture, and progressive filmmakers were working on transforming America going back to the immediate aftermath of World War II. Regardless their personal sins (and there were many), the movie studio heads of the 1930s and early 1940s knew their audience. Their audience was Middle America, the American Heartland, where families flocked to see films that affirmed their values, where good triumphed over evil, sacrifice trumped personal desire. Movie studio heads knew they alienated that audience at their peril.

The great movies of the period, such as *Casablanca*, dealt sensitively with issues of human temptation, but through implication and not through graphic portrayal. Yes, we all knew Rick and Ilsa loved each other, and something happened in Rick's room above his café when they were reunited, but eventually they chose to give up their personal desires for the greater good. The result was a powerful movie effectively portraying the meaning of personal sacrifice and redemption.

In fact, one commentator noted, "[With] *Casablanca* it is said that the Hollywood Production Code actually helped make the movie better. Instead of Rick and Ilsa ending up together (which would be adulterous), he sends her away."[18]

While many of these films were made by liberals, they still validated basic American ideals. But then a new breed of progressives came to Hollywood, the old movie moguls lost power by either dying or being forced out when television and other factors eroded their economic base, and American movies started to incrementally pursue a more progressive agenda.

Slowly, but surely, new movies from committed leftists such as Dore Schary (who took over MGM from staunch conservative Louis B. Mayer), John Huston, Richard Brooks, Stanley Kubrick, Stanley Kramer, and Elia Kazan promoted progressive attitudes on sexuality and economics.

Motion pictures could no longer merely entertain, they had to feature messages to convert the masses to progressive worldviews. And they had little or no concern about alienating Middle America. In fact, several reveled in doing so.

Now it would be foolhardy to elevate the old movie moguls as paragons of virtue, as the sordid tales of so-called "couch casting" (executives requiring sex from young actresses in return for promoting their careers), back-alley abortions, rampant sexual immorality, drug abuse, and other sordid practices have come to light via interviews and books on Hollywood's "Golden Era." Hollywood has always been anything but a model of virtue. To suggest otherwise would be an exercise in denial.

Like many others before the 1960s, these executives and others in the industry indulged in private sin while portraying public piety. But regardless of their private sins, they made sure (with a few notable exceptions) their movies never promoted, or celebrated, behaviors violating the core beliefs of faith, family, and patriotism held by most Americans. They knew their audience, and it was patriotic, churchgoing Americans.

However, starting in the late 1950s and then going full bore in the 1960s, filmmakers, such as those cited earlier, started to push the limits of the 1934 Production Code, which was instituted by the motion picture industry after backlash from religious groups and others about the risqué product (for that period) coming out of Hollywood in the late 1920s and early 1930s.

In addition, the slow collapse of the studio system, which had final say on released films, meant progressive filmmakers no longer had to be accountable for the content of the films they produced—even if it meant diminishing financial returns. By the 1960s, Hollywood had become a progressive bubble, and as politically and socially conservative performers and directors such as Clark Gable, Gary Cooper, Fred Astaire, Loretta Young, John Wayne, Jimmy Stewart, Frank Capra, and Leo McCarey, either died or were winding down their careers, they were replaced with a new breed of progressives for whom agenda trumped entertainment.

And by the early 1960s, these progressives were ready to challenge the production code—and challenge it in a big way with pushing the envelope sexually and with increasingly graphic violence.

Kubrick, for example, attempted to push through Hollywood's first full female nudity scene, featuring Jean Simmons, in the 1960 film *Spartacus*, but eventually was forced to darken certain areas of her anatomy so the nudity was implied and not shown.[19]

Not to be deterred, Kubrick chose to promote pedophilia in his 1962 film *Lolita* which features a professor played by James Mason becoming sexually infatuated with a young adolescent girl, played by then fourteen-year-old Sue Lyon. He goes as far as to marry the girl's mother in order to get access to the girl. Eventually, the mother dies after an argument with the professor, and it is implied he and the adolescent girl have a sexual encounter.

The only thing that kept *Lolita* from being worse was the still-in-place Production Code from the 1930s and efforts from the Catholic Legion of Decency. Kubrick would later lament, "because of all the pressure over the Production Code and the Catholic Legion of Decency at the time, I believe I didn't sufficiently dramatize the erotic aspect of Humbert's relationship with Lolita. If I could do the film over again, I would have stressed the erotic component of their relationship. . . ."[20]

By 1968, the Production Code was gone, and any prohibition on screen nudity, even among pre-adults, was removed. Licentiousness was now celebrated and seen as the ideal, while piety was to be mocked.

For instance, 1971's *The Last Picture Show*—featuring full frontal teenage male and female nudity, an autistic boy engaging in sexual relations with a prostitute, a teenage boy sleeping with a much older woman, and other forms of graphic sexuality—was hailed as a "classic" with little concern about what was being portrayed on screen. In 1969, *Midnight Cowboy* would become the first (and only) X-rated film to win Best Picture, while films like *Five Easy Pieces* celebrated sexual immorality and polyamory.[21]

In 1968, director Franco Zeffirelli basically forced two teenagers, against their will according to them, to perform a nude scene in his adaptation of *Romeo and Juliet*, far from anything William Shakespeare ever intended. And this was just the beginning. It was quickly to become much worse, as the sexualization of children, and in particular teenage girls, hit its zenith in the late 1970s and early 1980s in films such as *Pretty Baby*, *The Blue Lagoon* (both with a pre-teen and early teen Brooke Shields, who has recently disclosed the trauma she suffered due to her on-screen sexualization), *Fast Times at Ridgemont High* (1984), and more egregiously, *Blame It on Rio* (1984) which featured frequent nudity by an underage seventeen-year-old actress whose character ultimately engages in sexual relations with her father's middle-aged best friend. It made *Lolita* seem tame in comparison.

While "Me-Too" might have always been part of Hollywood, it was put on steroids in the 1960s.

And Americans greeted this all with a collective shrug, and in some cases, critical acclaim. What was unspeakable to be portrayed onscreen before the 1960s was now applauded and celebrated, and no boundary was left uncrossed.

But it was not just sex and nudity appearing on movie screens. Attacks on faith did as well. In the same year as *Spartacus*, 1960, Richard Brooks released *Elmer Gantry*, with Burt Lancaster, Jean Simmons, and Shirley Jones which focused on the seedy world of a corrupt evangelist and portrayed Christians as gullible fools. Also released that year was Kramer's *Inherit the Wind*, which, in its depiction of the infamous Scopes Monkey Trial, also portrayed Christians who believe in the creation story as ignorant rural backward buffoons, easy pickings for the enlightened elites promoting evolution to mock and ridicule.

The days of movies about benevolent priests, such as those played by Bing Crosby in *Going My Way* and *The Bells of St. Mary's*, or stalwart faithful ministers as in the biography of Peter Marshall in 1955's *A Man Called Peter*, were long gone. Faith was now to be vilified instead of celebrated because faith stood in the way of an "anything goes" society without moral restraints.

And as Saul Alinsky pointed out, "Ridicule is a powerful weapon," and Hollywood used ridicule, starting in the 1960s via the entertainment industry, to transform America's views on faith, and in particular biblical Christianity.

By the late 1960s, Hollywood seemed to mock everything good about America, while elevating anything portraying America in a negative light. Our entertainment quickly turned to mocking the normal while promoting the deviant. The Kinsey Report, which I mentioned earlier in the book, became the "Bible" for the entertainment world to follow—promoting all forms of sexual behavior while attacking traditional marriage and the family. Films such as *Bob & Carol & Ted & Alice* celebrated polyamory—couples engaging in open marriages by swapping sexual partners. *Myra Breckenridge* promoted practically every form of sexual behavior, with the nearly octogenarian Mae West making crude sexual come-ons throughout.

In less than ten years, Hollywood went from portraying married couples in separate beds to glorifying all forms of sexual behavior in the bedroom and in some cases, those married couples were seen as the aberration instead of the norm.

The 1960s also saw the glorification of criminals in films such as *Bonnie and Clyde*. Meanwhile, attempts to show military bravery, such as John Wayne's *The Green Berets*, were hooted and hollered out by the new elite running America's studios while movies such as 1969's *M*A*S*H*, directed by far-leftist Robert Altman, openly questioned America's involvement in the Korean War and depicted religion and the American military in a contemptable manner. The above-mentioned TV show by the same name was just a softer and gentler version of the movie's vitriol.

It was also in the 1960s when graphic violence became commonplace on screen in films such as Stanley Kubrick's *A Clockwork Orange* and Sam Peckinpaugh's *The Wild Bunch*. These films glamorized violence and desensitized film audiences, to the willful destruction of human life. It is no coincidence our society became more violent as Hollywood became more violent.

Because movies were something you had to purchase a ticket to go and see, the progressive movement was more limited in their ability to make advancements there at first. People could choose not to go see these films or allow their children to see these films. And a lot of Americans chose not to go, limiting the influence of progressives at the movie theaters initially.

But once television, through Norman Lear and others, started to go the same route and brought their agendas into American homes via television sets, progressives had a captive audience, including children, to influence and corrupt.

That is why the influence of Norman Lear, and other progressives, was more insidious and influential once they took over television. Americans, especially children, could no longer escape the progressive entertainment agenda.

HUGH HEFNER AND PLAYBOY

Another entry point to American homes for the progressive sexual agenda was through Hugh Hefner's *Playboy* magazine—which started in the 1950s, thanks to the Kinsey Report, but then exploded in the 1960s—and its normalization of pornography and misogyny through the promotion of the "Playboy Philosophy."

By creating air-brushed images of perfect women for men to lust over, Hefner's magazine damaged or destroyed countless marriages as men became disenchanted with their less-than-physically-perfect wives. In addition, it fueled pornography addiction, serving as a gateway, just like drugs through releasing dopamine and re-wiring the brain, to harder and harder core material to bring "satisfaction."

Hugh Hefner said it was the research of Dr. Alfred Kinsey that inspired him to create *Playboy*. Hefner wrote in the first issue, "We believe . . . we are filling a publishing need only slightly less important than one just taken care of by the Kinsey Report."[22]

It has only been recently, after Hefner's death, people have started to critically look at his legacy. Several of the women he exploited for his and others' personal sexual pleasure have come forward with horror stories of what occurred in the infamous Playboy Mansion. Others have spoken out about how his "Playboy Philosophy" has led to sexual abuse, pornography addiction, disrespect for women, female body image issues leading to anorexia and bulimia, and other social pathologies.[23] While Hefner may be dead, his philosophy, which took root in the 1960s, continues to haunt young women, destroy young men, and fuel distrust among the sexes along sexual lines.

The "Playboy Philosophy" took what was previously behind locked doors because of fear and rightful shame and brought it out into the open for all to see and celebrate. It flipped the script, ridiculing those who believed in treating women with dignity and respect, while celebrating the sexual exploitation of others for personal profit and "pleasure."

Yes, there was pornography before Hefner and *Playboy*, and sexual lust and hedonism has existed as long as human beings have roamed this earth. But by making access to pornographic material more socially acceptable and "respectable," Hefner created an increasingly unsafe environment for younger women, in particular, as his philosophy gave older men a green light to pursue them sexually.

As Mary Eberstadt writes, "In 1953, when the first issue of *Playboy* arrived on newsstands, many people wanted to believe its hype about enhancing the sophistication and urbanity of American men. By today, it is harder to pretend the mainstreaming of pornography has been anything but a disaster for romance, and a prime factor in today's breakups and social consumerism."[24]

Despite Hefner's destructive influence, the Chicago City Council voted in 2000 to rename a street in his "honor." The council said it was their way of thanking Hefner for keeping his Playboy headquarters in the city. In acknowledging the honor, Hefner's daughter Christie, called her father "the quintessential American success story."[25]

This decision by the City Council to honor a man who sexually exploited women, destroyed marriages, and encouraged men to be as sexually promiscuous as possible without accepting responsibility for their actions, shows how deeply the sexual ethos of the 1960s, as expressed through nearly every aspect of the entertainment industry, infected our culture.

Thus, while we probably would still have notorious misogynists like Andrew Tate, or sexual predators who pay off student debt for young women in exchange for sexual trysts via websites such as Seeking Arrangement, their behaviors would not be defended, or seen as a role model for other men, without Hefner's influence. The "Playboy Philosophy" gave them the cultural approval to not only pursue their most carnal urges, but to do so with a good deal of cultural celebration as well.

The "Playboy Philosophy" that first emerged in the 1950s was coupled with the pill and legalized abortion and came to fruition with the sexual revolution of the 1960s, leaving a deadly and destructive trail of broken bodies and spirits in its wake.

WOODSTOCK

Besides the cultural transformations facilitated by movies, television, and magazines, another entertainment transformation occurred in the 1960s: the glorification of illegal drug use, rebellion, and "anything goes" sexual behavior through popular music. The epitome of this movement is the famous, and in many ways infamous, Woodstock Music Festival in August 1969.

Woodstock took place on a 49-acre dairy farm in New York State. It had been anticipated about 50,000 would attend a three-day music concert—billed as "Three Days of Music and Peace" and headlined by the major countercultural bands of the day.

While tickets were sold in advance for $18 (or $6.50 per day), and $24 at the gate, newspaper, magazine, and radio advertisements, along with word-of-mouth publicity, ended up inspiring more than 400,000 people to show up. Unprepared for the massive crowd and the ticket sales for such a throng, the organizers were forced to make the event free.

Woodstock still holds an almost mythical status among those who attended—even those who have long since left their leftist, counterculture beliefs behind. As Marco Margaritoff wrote, "half a million hippies, beatniks, and long-hairs descended upon upstate New York for the Woodstock music festival. The world would never be the same."[25]

Woodstock was first billed as "An Aquarian Exposition," but soon devolved into rampant drug use, random sex, and nudity. As one attendee noted, 'I'm pretty sure there was a cloud of marijuana over the whole area. I enjoyed the whole show but I'm pretty sure I was a little altered. And I did have some champagne that they handed down from the stage. So that was cool. I'd never had champagne before.'"[26]

While music was being played onstage, a lot of sex was happening off stage. As one observer noted, "It's no surprise that many attendees birthed children some nine months later."[27]

Three people lost their lives at Woodstock. Two died from drug overdoses and another was run over by a tractor while he was sleeping. Eight women suffered miscarriages. The New York State Department of Health eventually recorded 5,162 medical incidents—of which 800 were drug-related—over the four days of the event.[28]

Another observer, then twenty-two-year-old Joey Reynolds recalls, "There was a lot of drug stuff—overdoses, acting out, puking and drinking."[29]

Yet, despite the debauchery, Woodstock was celebrated, and is still celebrated, by many. Forgotten is how many of the performers, such as Janis Joplin and Jimi Hendrix, died soon afterward from drug overdoses.

Ultimately, Woodstock was a very tragic event—because it played a pivotal role in fully ushering in the ethos of the 1960s taking root in the 1970s and beyond—and doomed millions of young people to death by drug overdose, unwed parenthood, and rebellion. What was being celebrated was not "peace and love" but ultimately "death and destruction" for not only one generation but generations to come.

Four months after Woodstock, another "event" was held at the Altamont Speedway in Northern California. It was hardly a celebration of peace and love, and it exposed the ugly side of the 1960s' hippie culture. Headlined by the Rolling Stones, it was described by Owen Gleiberman of the BBC as "the rock dream turned nightmare, the official last nail in the coffin of the '60s."[30]

While the Rolling Stones performed their set, a member of the California Hells Angels, a violent motorcycle gang that was hired instead of off-duty police or regular guards to provide security, stabbed and murdered a young man named Meredith Hunter who was strung out on drugs.

Gleiberman writes, "Altamont was all about 'the devil' showing his face to put an end to the peace-and-love generation. When you watch *Gimme Shelter*, the great 1970 documentary that caught the dark tumult of Altamont on film, the fights that break out in the audience, with roiling rows of spectators backing off from the violence in waves, seem to channel an ominous energy that is almost ghostly."[31]

He concludes, "Nearly half a century later, it's automatic to think of Altamont as the end of something. Yet it now looks like the beginning of something too: a world in which the aggression of the self, on the part of just about everybody, would be given a new license. The '60s, after all, are long gone, and perhaps they really did die that day. But the violence and chaos that ruled Altamont don't look trapped in the past. They look all too present."

His words are unfortunately all too true. The entertainment culture of the 2020s is just a reflection of what was unleashed on America in the 1960s via television, movies, magazines, and concerts. When you coarsen the culture, an entire nation devolves into Altamonts—complete with violence, disrespect, and ultimately tragedy.

So many of our current social ills can be attributed directly to the takeover of the entertainment industry in the 1960s. Hollywood elites decided to no longer entertain the masses but preach to them, and then condemn the masses when they responded and acted upon what was being pumped into their living rooms, theaters, and concerts— graphic violence, premarital sex, adultery, to name just a few.

That is the sad entertainment legacy given to us by the 1960s. And as it has been said "law follows culture." Through its concerted effort to transform American culture, the entertainment industry was able to radically change every American institution, including the law, public policy, and the family as well.

CHAPTER SIX

The Fiscal Stumble

Viewed from today's perspective, the Great Society seems to have been above all an almost preposterously bloated collection of social-engineering projects. The mentality that underlay this panoply of policies and actions was one of arrogance and presumption: the presupposition that the leadings intellectuals, "the best and the brightest," ought to, and knew how to rearrange the pieces on the human chess board to construct a better society from the top down.[1]

—Robert Higgs

In 1960, our national debt was $286 billion. While that amount of debt is lamentable, it is nothing compared to today's debt. In 2023, the outstanding national debt was over $32 trillion and continues to grow at an alarming rate.[2] As I write, the president and Congress have engaged in another one of their brinkmanship sessions over raising the national debt ceiling so the government can continue to spend like a bank robber with little or no concern about when the consequences will eventually arrive.

Meanwhile, despite this massive debt, our roads and bridges are crumbling away, our armed forces are dealing with rapidly aging equipment, and we are repeating the mistakes of history by thinking if we just print enough money, we can make the problem go away.

How did we get to this point? The primary culprit is progressive fiscal policies, first started under Franklin Roosevelt and the New Deal of 1930s, but exacerbated by the progressive policies of the 1960s as, flush from one of the greatest landslides in presidential election history, President Lyndon Johnson ushered in his utopian "Great Society" programs in 1965, which I will discuss in depth.

In a misguided effort to alleviate poverty (which instead exacerbated it), President Johnson, emboldened with strong liberal majorities in Congress launched a series of expensive domestic spending programs designed to alleviate poverty. He also tried to have what has been called "guns and butter" by greatly increasing military spending to pay for American involvement in the Vietnam War.

The result? Steady, and then dramatic rises in wages and prices, which fueled the inflation cycle of the 1970s and beyond. Inflation in 1960 was 1.39 percent. By 1970, it was 5.29 percent. By 1979, it was 13.29 percent.[3] This became known as the "misery index."

The apex was the "stagflation" era of Jimmy Carter's presidency, with sky-high inflation and interest rates, which not only made life more difficult for those on the bottom of the economic ladder, but financially crippled the middle class as well.[4]

THE GREAT (MISGUIDED) SOCIETY

In his January 1964 State of the Union address, Johnson outlined his utopian hopes that ultimately lead to despair. He said, "This administration today, here and now, declares unconditional war on poverty."[5]

A few months later, on May 24, 1964, Johnson gave another speech at the University of Michigan where he laid out his lofty plans, which he dubbed "The Great Society." He said:

> The Great Society rests on abundance and liberty for all. It demands an end to poverty and racial injustice, to which we are totally committed in our time. But that is just the beginning.
>
> The Great Society is a place where every child can find knowledge to enrich his mind and to enlarge his talents. It is a place where leisure is a welcome chance to build and reflect, not a feared cause of boredom and restlessness. It is a place where the city of man serves not only the needs of the body and the demands of commerce but the desire for beauty and the hunger for community.
>
> It is a place where man can renew contact with nature. It is a place which honors creation for its own sake and for what it adds to the understanding of the race. It is a place where men are more concerned with the quality of their goals than the quantity of their goods.
>
> But most of all, the Great Society is not a safe harbor, a resting place, a final objective, a finished work. It is a challenge constantly renewed, beckoning us toward a destiny where the meaning of our lives matches the marvelous products of our labor.[6]

Johnson went on in his speech to discuss the ills he believed America was suffering from: decaying urban centers, an underachieving educational system, and a blighted environment.

Unfortunately, instead of solving these problems, the Great Society would only make them worse.

Why? Because regardless of how noble his intentions may have been (and up for debate), Johnson and his allies in Congress, through the Great Society, declared unconditional war on lower- and middle-class Americans. After spending nearly $22 trillion in their "war on poverty," Johnson's administration achieved little or no progress, and in some cases, made poverty even worse. As the Heritage Foundation wrote in their 2014 report commemorating the 50th anniversary of Johnson's speech, "In fact, a significant portion of the population is now less capable of self-sufficiency than it was when the War on Poverty began."[7]

The utopian premise behind the Great Society was based on the arrogant belief that the poor needed to be protected by the elite who supposedly knew better how to solve the problems of the lower class. Thus, government needed to swoop in and become a sort of daycare center for the poor, pushing people into a one-size-fits-all federal nanny program ultimately nothing more than a substitute for equipping people with the skills they needed to succeed in life.

So, instead of private programs such as apprenticeships teaching young people a solid work ethic and marketable skill, they were pushed into government job programs that often didn't provide any such transferable skill. The Great Society transformed our society from one which would lend a hand to help someone succeed in life to one teaching them to keep their hand out and engage in behavior eventually dooming them to failure.

And American fiscal responsibility has never been the same since—with trillions of dollars wasted in an effort that has only made the problem it was supposed to solve much worse. One only needs to visit America's inner cities to see the evidence of that.

As noted by the National Taxpayers Union Foundation, the federal government posted surpluses in twenty-three years during the first half of the twentieth century.[8] This is amazing, given the massive spending required to enact Franklin Roosevelt's "New Deal" and then to fight and win World War II.

However, the second half of the twentieth century, which includes the 1960s and beyond, netted only seven surpluses. The Heritage Foundation concludes, "As deficits reach progressively higher levels, they could become millstones around the neck of future taxpayers in the form of higher taxes, slower economic growth, and higher interest payments on the ever-growing federal debt."[9]

The Heritage Foundation reports the government spends sixteen times more, adjusting for inflation, on means-tested welfare or anti-poverty programs than it did when the War on Poverty started. But as welfare spending soared, the decline in poverty, which was occurring before the so-called Great Society reforms, stopped, and in many cases reversed directions and became worse.[10]

For instance, in 1962, according to the Congressional Research Services, three years before the Great Society began, mandatory spending was only 30 percent of the federal budget. It is currently nearly 60 percent and continues to rise. On their current trajectory, spending on health care, Social Security, and interest on the national debt will consume all federal tax revenues by 2045, leaving nothing left over for "discretionary" but necessary programs such as defense and medical research.[11]

In 2021, health care analyst Sally Pipes of the Pacific Research Institute reported that two years after Medicare was implemented in 1964, the House Ways and Means Committee forecast it would cost $12 billion by 1990.[12] The actual figure ended up being nearly ten times more— $110 billion.[13] In 2021, Medicare spending hit $875 billion, and will be over $1 trillion by 2030 as Baby Boomers and the oldest members of Generation X start to swarm the system.[14]

Laura Hollis writes, "Medicaid has had a similar trajectory. It cost taxpayers $3 billion in 1967, when slightly less than 4% of the U.S. population was enrolled. As of February 2022, 87 million people were receiving Medicaid or CHIP (Children's Health Insurance Program) benefits—26% of the population, or more than one in every four Americans. Medicaid spending in 2021 was $696 billion. Of that, $86 billion (that we know of) was squandered on fraud or other 'improper payments.'"[15] Together Medicare and Medicaid now cost nearly $1 trillion annually, and along with Social Security at more than $19 trillion, are the main causes of our national debt.[16]

Besides federal deficits reaching tens of trillions of dollars that will eventually cripple future generations, the Great Society gave men and women a blank check to evade responsibility for their actions—creating a society of fatherless children and government-dependent mothers.

Robert Higgs writes, "Under Johnson, however, the federal government's intrusion into economic life swelled enormously."[17] Paul Conkin notes, "In little more than two years after LBJ took office, Congress enacted over two hundred major bills and at least a dozen landmark measures. The ferment, the chaos, rivaled that of 1933, and all at a scope at least four times greater than the early New Deal."[18]

He adds: "In five years the American government approximately doubled its regulatory role and at least doubled the scope of transfer payments."[19]

According to Henry J. Aaron, "No administration since Franklin Roosevelt's first had operated subject to fewer political constraints than President Johnson's."[20] And without constraints, there was no accountability, and progressives had a "blank check" to write their desired amount on, even if there were not enough funds to cover their spending.

Like many government solutions, the Great Society showed promising initial results before reality started to sink in. In the first six years after its implementation, self-sufficiency did rise. But that was an illusion, because as Rachel Sheffield and Robert Rector of the Heritage Foundation point out, it was not government spending lifting people out of poverty, instead it was rising wages and education levels.[21]

But in the late sixties and early seventies, things took a turn in the wrong direction, and Johnson's utopian plans turned large swaths of America into stagnant and declining abysses. The result is a large portion of the American population are less self-sufficient than when the War on Poverty began.

Why? Because the vast expansion of the welfare state eroded the work ethic and family structure of American society.

Regarding work ethic, the Great Society diminished self-sufficiency by giving financial rewards for not working or for working less than people used to. In many cases, it became more profitable not to work. The result is similar to the following comedic exchange between Chico and Groucho from the Marx Brothers' 1930 film, *Animal Crackers*:

Chico: Oh, for playing, we get ten dollars an hour.

Groucho: I see. What do you get for *not* playing?

Chico: Twelve dollars an hour.

Groucho: Well, clip me off a piece of that.

Chico: Now for rehearsing, we make special rate: that's a fifteen dollars an hour.

Groucho: That's for *rehearsing*?

Chico: That's for rehearsing.

Groucho: And what do you get for *not* rehearsing?

Chico: You couldn't afford it. You see, if we don't rehearse, we don't play. And if we don't play *[snaps fingers]*, that runs into money.[22]

As Rector states, "The low level of parental work is a major cause of official child poverty and the lack of self-sufficiency. Even in good economic times, the median poor family with children has only 1,000 hours of parental work per year. This is the equivalent of one adult working 20 hours per week. If the amount of work performed in poor families with children was increased to the equivalent of one adult working full-time through the year, the poverty rate among these families would drop by two-thirds."[23]

So we end up with a society that is paying people, like Chico in *Animal Crackers*, more to not work than to work!

I will discuss the ramifications of the breakdown of the family caused by Great Society "reforms" in a forthcoming chapter, but Sheffield and Rector put it succinctly:

The War on Poverty crippled marriage in low-income communities. As means-tested benefits were expanded, welfare began to serve as a substitute for a husband in the home, eroding marriage among lower-income Americans. In addition, the welfare system penalized low-income couples who did marry by eliminating or substantially reducing benefits. As husbands left the home, the need for more welfare to support single mothers increased. The War on Poverty created a destructive feedback loop: Welfare promoted the decline of marriage, which generated the need for more welfare.[24]

Sheffield and Rector conclude, "The lack of progress in self-sufficiency is due in major part to the welfare system itself. Welfare wages war on social capital, breaking down the habits and norms that lead to self-reliance, especially those of marriage and work. It thereby generates a pattern of increasing intergenerational dependence."[25]

Meanwhile, Great Society programs, as noted earlier, through the creation of new entitlement spending programs beyond Social Security, now encompass a large percentage of our government spending, while our infrastructure crumbles away.

One only needs to take a ride on the Pennsylvania Railroad from Washington D.C. to New York City to see the rotting infrastructure and tragic poverty of poor communities at the various stops along the way to observe the devastation that has occurred. A train ride that used to be the subject of joyous songs is now a dirge of despair.

The result is not only crippling national debt and the continued failure of government to solve the problems it created (and has exacerbated), but also increasing economic pressures on the middle class through higher taxes and increasing regulation—widening the gap between the "haves" and "have nots." This is in alignment with the goals of Saul Alinsky.

As Amity Shlaes, the author of *Great Society: A New History*, points out, "To pay for its Great Society commitments, the U.S. government in the next decade found itself forced to set taxes so high that it further suppressed the commercialization of innovation."[26] And with tax rates, both corporate and private, raised so high to pay for the Great Society, American technological development ground to a halt and American families found it harder and harder to make ends meet—thus the Great Society hurt the very people it purported to help.

Shlaes adds, "In fact, what the War on Poverty and the new flood of benefits did do was the opposite of prevent [poverty]—they established a new kind of poverty, a permanent sense of downtroddenness."[27]

But that is what socialism does, whether it be in Venezuela or in the Communist Bloc countries in the days of the old Soviet Union. According to Shlaes, the Great Society was built on a socialist platform, with one person, Michael Harrington, who was part of the *Port Huron Statement* mentioned earlier, playing a significant role in shaping the Great Society "reforms."[28] While Harrington was no fan of Soviet communism and was seen as one of the more moderate members of the *Port Huron Statement* draftees, his presence showed the influence members of that group were starting to achieve in the federal government.

And it was not just Lyndon Johnson who fueled the runaway train of government spending through his Great Society programs. His successor, Richard Nixon, a Republican, grew total annual entitlement spending 20 percent faster than Johnson's administration.[29] Once the dam of fiscal restraint was removed, government spending quickly became an out-of-control flood no one, not even Ronald Reagan, could halt.

As Shlaes puts it, "In its Great Society endeavor, the country relegated the private sector to the role of consultant, workhouse, and milk cow."[30] She adds, "Those on the far left who had originally pushed for aggressive public-sector expansion had achieved what they sought, to subordinate the private sector."[31]

She concludes, "Today . . . the 1960s are catching up with us. Medicare and Medicaid, undertakings that sounded reasonable at a time when life expectancy was lower, now cost the country trillions it cannot afford. Younger generations can expect no pensions: the budget of Social Security, the national pension fund expanded so dramatically in the 1960s, will be exhausted before it is time for those generations to retire."[32]

And what have we gotten for this massive spending and mortgaging of our children's future? Very little.

One example is Head Start, one of the Great Society initiatives. Meant to be a federal pre-kindergarten program to help low-income children, it has produced no lasting improvements for those children. The federal government has spent more than $240 billion since 1965 on this program and realized little to zero return on investment. But the $240 billion spent on Head Start is chump change compared to what the government has spent on K-12 education which produces increasingly dismal results with each passing year. Great Society education "reforms" have cost taxpayers $2 trillion with no educational improvement. In fact, a case can be made that education has grown worse, especially for low-income children trapped in corrupt inner-city schools.

Meanwhile, federal government student loan programs have made college more expensive for everyone and virtually unattainable for lower-class families, as over the past thirty-five years, tuition has increased 237 percent after accounting for inflation. As Lindsey Burke of the Heritage Foundation has noted, a slightly *smaller* proportion of students from families in the bottom quartile of the income distribution graduate from college today, the very students Johnson's loan programs were supposed to help.[33]

As anyone who has finally come to grips with denial of fiscal reality and rampant overspending realizes, there comes a point when all the credit is exhausted, there is no more money to be borrowed, and the creditors are pounding at the door. That is the scenario we, as a nation, are bequeathing future generations thanks to the fiscal policies of the past sixty years. Meanwhile, we continue to charge the national credit card, asking for and getting credit line increases, so we can continue on our national binge.

So the ultimate result of the 1960s' drunken spending spree is an increasingly crumbling infrastructure, parental irresponsibility, greater poverty, stagnant or even poorer education, massive government deficits, and the exacerbation of the problems the spending was supposed to solve. And like Chico tells Groucho in *Animal Crackers*, ultimately "we can't afford it."

That's the fiscal nightmare we are in, thanks to the 1960s. And it's the nightmare that will impact the future of our children and grandchildren when the bill finally comes due.

CHAPTER SEVEN

The Family Stumble

Despite the grand myth that black economic progress began or accelerated with the passage of the civil rights laws and "war on poverty" programs of the 1960s, the cold fact is that the poverty rate among blacks fell from 87 percent in 1940 to 47 percent by 1960. This was before any of those programs began. . . . Nearly a hundred years of the supposed "legacy of slavery" found most black children being raised in two-parent families in 1960. But thirty years after the liberal welfare state found the great majority of black children being raised by a single parent. . . . The murder rate among blacks in 1960 was one-half of what it became 20 years later, after a legacy of liberals' law enforcement policies.[1]

—Thomas Sowell

Prior to the late 1960s, Americans were more likely to look at marriage and family through the prisms of duty, obligation, and sacrifice. A successful, happy home was one in which intimacy was an important good, but by no means the only one in view. A decent job, a well-maintained home, mutual spousal aid, child-rearing, and shared religious faith were seen almost universally as the goods that marriage and family life were intended to advance. But the psychological revolution's focus on individual fulfillment and personal growth changed all that. Increasingly, marriage was seen as a vehicle for a self-oriented ethic of romance, intimacy, and fulfillment.[2]

—W. Bradford Wilcox

U p until the 1960s, the traditional nuclear family—one man, one woman, and at least one child—was seen as the societal ideal. But in the 1960s, the American family came under withering attack and has never been the same since.

The Great Society, as discussed in the last chapter, took a wrecking ball to the African American family as men no longer had to be responsible for the children they fathered as long as the government was there to subsidize their promiscuity. No-fault divorce laws were proposed, under the pretense of making divorce more amicable and less traumatic, and the result was a skyrocketing divorce rate and generations of devastated children.

The entertainment industry, as discussed earlier, mocked the family, particularly fathers, in shows such as *All in the Family*, *Maude*, *Soap*, and others. Coupling this with Hugh Hefner's "Playboy Philosophy," many feminists declared war on all men—regardless of their innocence or guilt—for misogynist behavior.

The march toward legalized abortion only made such behavior worse as men no longer had to take responsibility for the children they fathered. The "problem" could just be dispensed of by going to your local Planned Parenthood or local abortion clinic. When informed of an unplanned pregnancy, many a woman heard the words, "Just kill it."

In 1960, 73 percent of children lived in a traditional two-parent never-divorced home, headed by a father and a mother. By 1980, that percentage dropped to 61 percent and by 2015, it dropped to 46 percent.[3]

Sadly, some children grew up in broken or troubled homes before the 1960s. But they tended to be the exception instead of the rule, and even troubled homes often had the presence of both a mother and father. The sexual ethos of the 1960s turned what was the exception into the rule.

Why has this occurred? According to Alicia VanOrman and Linda A. Jacobsen of the Population Reference Bureau,

"Beginning in the 1960s—and accelerating over the last two decades—changes in marriage, cohabitation, and childbearing have played a key role in transforming household composition in the United States."[4]

A 2016 study done by VanOrman and her co-author Paola Scommegna provides a stark look of the societal wreckage the 1960s unleashed on the family. They found the radical changes of the 1960s led to more children growing up poor and more adults reaching old age without either a spouse or ties to an adult child to provide care—and thus finding themselves more dependent on the government.

Ron Haskins, writing for the center-Left Brookings Institute, describes how the Great Society exacerbated the real issue behind poverty: the dissolution of the family. He wrote:

> Changes in family composition are also deeply implicated in the stubbornness of poverty. Kids in single-parent families are about five times as likely to be poor as children in married-couple families. Yet the share of children in single-parent families has been rising for decades. Worse, poor and poorly educated adults are much more likely to have nonmarital births than wealthier and better educated adults, creating another pathway for the intergenerational transmission of poverty. Equally important, children reared in single-parent families are more likely to have education and behavioral problems than children from married-couple families, further increasing the likelihood that the children will be poor as adults.[5]

He concludes:

> To mount an effective war against poverty, we need changes in the personal decisions of more young Americans. Unless young people get more education,

work more, and stop having babies outside marriage, government spending will be minimally effective in fighting poverty. On the other hand, providing government support to increase the incentives and payoff for low-income jobs and redesigning the nation's · welfare programs to encourage marriage hold great promise for at last achieving the poverty reduction envisioned by President Johnson.[6]

The rejection of traditional morality in the 1960s, accelerated by the Great Society programs, has led to a consistent drop in the prevalence of marriage. This has manifested itself through young adults delaying marriage, choosing to cohabitate instead of marrying, or having trouble making commitments because of previous trauma, such as the loss of a parent through divorce—which was weaponized through the no-fault divorce laws of the late 1960s. And as a result, poverty, as we have seen and will see, has increased instead of decreased.

For instance, cohabitation now makes up the majority of first-time, live-in romantic relationships between men and women. Unfortunately, cohabitation often results in short and unstable relationships, often with negative emotional consequences for at least one of the parties. And cohabitation has also resulted in the postponement of marriage as only about two out of five cohabiting couples marry within three years.

And, as previously noted, cohabitation affects children as an ever-growing share of children have moved from families with two biological parents to ones headed by a single parent, or with a cohabiting parent or a stepparent. Numerous research studies have shown children not raised in stable, two-biological-parent homes are more likely to be poor, underperform academically, and receive lower-quality parenting—all factors that can negatively impact their lives.

THE TOLL ON AFRICAN AMERICAN HOMES

And who has suffered the most from the ethos of the sexual revolution and the subsequent decline in marriage? Those living in poverty in our inner cities, and those with lower education levels. Many of the policies of the 1960s, sadly, set the African American community back with regard to economic and social advancement. In addition, radicals hijacked what was good—the civil rights movement—to advance other agendas that divided, rather than unified America, and had little or nothing to do with actual discrimination.

That is why the toll of the progressive ethos that took root in the 1960s has been especially harsh on African American homes. In 1965, at the height of the Johnson administration and its Great Society programs, one classically liberal senator, Daniel Patrick Moynihan of New York, raised the alarm at the decay he was already seeing.

The huge infusion of federal spending, as chronicled in the previous chapter, led to tragic ramifications for marriage, family, and American society as a whole. America's inner cities, already crumbling in 1965, have now dissolved into chaos and despair over the succeeding fifty-plus years as the mistakes made in the 1960s, like compound interest in a bank account, continue to multiply.

Moynihan released a report, *The Negro Family: The Case for National Action*, because he was deeply concerned about the seemingly endless cycle of poverty in the African American community. At the time of his report, about one-quarter of African American children were living in fatherless homes—a statistic Moynihan called a crisis. But what was a crisis in 1965 has become a full-out emergency and epidemic nearly sixty years later. By 2014, that percentage increased to 70 and has remained fairly constant at that percentage point ever since.

Moynihan later stated the Great Society era "gave great influence in social policy to viewpoints that rejected the proposition that family structure might be a social issue."[7] But as tragic as these numbers, and their implications are for the African American community, the progressive sexual ethos of the 1960s and the resulting policy failures of the Great Society enabling irresponsible behavior, have now infected all aspects of American family life. More than half of Hispanic children are born out of wedlock, as well as 27 percent of Caucasian children. Overall, 40 percent of all children are born to unwed mothers.[8]

Manhattan Institute Senior Fellow Jason Riley states that despite more than $22 trillion spent on so-called "Great Society" policies over the past fifty-plus years, four out of every five American children raised by a single mother live at or below the poverty line. In contrast, for married black Americans, the poverty rate is below 10 percent.[9]

Riley writes, "the likelihood of teen pregnancy, drug abuse, dropping out of school, and many other social problems grew dramatically when parents were absent."[10]

The irony is all these policies which have devastated minority communities were bequeathed by liberal political elites who entered the fray just as the underclass, and particularly the minority underclass, was beginning to rise and achieve success.

For example, until 1975, the racial gap in average earnings among full-time male workers in the United States narrowed. After 1970, racial convergence in earnings slowed markedly, in part because many low-wage black males were no longer engaged in full-time work, often because of the government subsidies provided by Johnson's Great Society reforms.[11]

In his seminal work on the disastrous policies of the 1960s, Myron Magnet writes:

In the sixties, just when the successes of the civil rights movement were removing racial barriers to mainstream opportunities, the mainstream values that poor blacks needed to seize those changes, values such as hard work and self-denial, came under sharp attack. Poor blacks needed all the support and encouragement that mainstream culture could give them to stand up and make their own fates. But mainstream culture let them down. Issuing the opposite of a call to responsibility and self-reliance, the larger culture told blacks in particular, and the poor in general, that they were victims, and that society, not they themselves, was responsible not only for their present but their future condition.[12]

That sense of victimhood, and hopelessness, resulted in the end of the peaceful civil rights movement under the direction of Rev. Dr. Martin Luther King Jr., and to the destructive race riots in Harlem, Watts, Newark, and Detroit—to name just a few. These riots, often encouraged and assisted by progressives, further devastated America's inner cities, destroyed property values, and increased criminal activities even more than before.

Thus, that depressing view out the train window of crumbling buildings, abject poverty, and urban blight between Washington, D.C. and New York City continues to be brought to you by the policies and behaviors of the 1960s and its destructive impact on poor inner-city African American families.

SUBSIDIZING COHABITATION WHILE DISCOURAGING MARRIAGE

In addition to the Great Society and the devastating effects it had on the family, other societal forces were in play. The development and legalization of birth control, and later abortion, created a culture where sexual activity outside of marriage exploded. And just as government spending attempted to remove the fiscal responsibility inhibiting such choices, birth control and abortion allowed men to avoid responsibility for the children they fathered.

Herbert Marcuse would be pleased.

But ultimately, the Great Society turbo-charged the breakdown of family, and the negative ramifications for society, by creating government policies that penalized marriage, instead of encouraging it.

Paul Peterson of Harvard University states, "Some programs actively discouraged marriage. . . . [Since] welfare assistance went to mothers so long as no male was boarding in the household . . . marriage to an employed male, even one earning the minimum wage, placed at risk a mother's economic well-being."[13]

Peterson adds, it was said by 1975, a head of household had to earn an estimated $20,000 a year to have more resources than could be obtained through Great Society programs. That's equal to an annual $90,000 today.[14]

How so? Means-tested tax and transfer programs, which were implemented as part of the so-called "reforms" of the Great Society, actually penalize marriage among low-income families. Why? Because unmarried couples lose critical federal support and tax benefits if they choose to get married. If they remain unmarried, they will continue to get those benefits.

Another Harvard professor Steven Pinker agrees, "A large proportion (today a majority) of black children are born out of wedlock, and many grow up without fathers. This trend, already visible in the early 1960s, may have been multiplied by the sexual revolution and yet again by perverse welfare incentives that encouraged young women to "marry the state" instead of the fathers of their children."[15]

Thus, even if the utopian ideal of the Great Society was to keep families together, its policies and their implementation did the exact opposite by giving incentives to encourage irresponsibility and family fragmentation.

The American Enterprise Institute (AEI) documented this in a study finding a pregnant woman earning $21,000 a year who chooses to cohabitate with a man making $29,000 a year, would likely be eligible to receive money from the Medicaid/Child's Health Insurance Plan, known as CHIP.[16]

However, if they choose to get married, their combined income of $50,000 a year makes her ineligible for coverage for childbirth and associated prenatal care, which has an estimated annual cost of $12,000.

The result? The government, through policies implemented in the 1960s, has made it financially beneficial for the couple not to marry! As Jason Riley states, "The government paid mothers to keep fathers out of the home—and paid them well."[17]

This outcome was best illustrated when in 2016 AEI asked men and women who lived below the poverty line if they would choose to not get married out of fear of losing welfare benefits. Of those surveyed, 24 percent responded "almost always" and 23 percent said "often."[18]

This is again the consequence of the intellectual and policy bankruptcy of Lyndon Johnson's Great Society reforms of the 1960s which created these subsidies. And these subsidies are the "gift that keeps on giving" with regard to encouraging cohabitation instead of marriage. As lower-income families take advantage of multiple means-tested benefits, the temptation to not get married only grows stronger. These cohabitating couples now face even more marriage penalties—only accelerating the decline of stable families amongst those with less education and opportunity.

DEMOGRAPHIC SUICIDE

But the family has not just come under attack through the
Great Society programs of the 1960s. It has also come under
attack through the overall secularization of society that
began in the 1960s.

During the 1960s, population doomsayers like the late
Paul Ehrlich spread a message that people were procreating
too much and people must stop having babies in order to
"save the planet."[19] These doomsayers saw religious Americans as the main culprit because they were perceived to be
more likely to have large families.

Thus, if your religion is "saving the planet," in the mind
of these doomsayers, you need to attack the faith you perceive is causing harm to the planet.

But without faith to preach selflessness, societies become
selfish. Since successful marriages and families require self-
sacrifice, societies start to experience the ramifications of
turning away from God not just through rising divorce rates
and willful disregard for children, but also on their demographic future. With faith diminished, the very fabric making
up a healthy family is torn, and people start to have fewer
children for countless secular and selfish reasons.

In the most extreme manifestations of this mindset,
children are seen as either impediments to personal fulfillment or, in the case of radical environmentalists, "destructive" to the future of the planet.

For example, the newest generation of doomsayers now
say people need to limit themselves to one child or no children to bring an end to "climate change." And, like those
in the 1960s, they often blame those who do not adhere to
their new religion of "climate change" for allowing their
religious beliefs to stop them from the "necessary sacrifice"
of not having children.

But without children, America is heading toward a demographic nightmare—one we are already seeing with fewer young Americans paying into government-run systems, such as Social Security and Medicare, meant to support older Americans. In addition, our current labor shortages are related to fewer able-bodied younger Americans entering the workforce.

Professor Christopher Murray, the director of the Institute for Health Metrics and Evaluation at the University of Washington, documents this coming demographic disaster. He and his team found the number of children under five will fall from 681 million worldwide in 2017 to 401 million in 2100, while the number of over-eighty-year-olds will rise from 141 million in 2017 to 866 million in 2100.[20]

One report shows the American birthrate is at the lowest it has been in four decades, and the fertility rate is the lowest it has been since the 1930s.[21] This is not a new trajectory, as many of these declines began with the paradigm shift of the 1960s. A paradigm shift, as mentioned before, leading to legalized abortion (and the deaths of more than sixty million innocent children), and other scientific and social forces meant to limit the number of children in society, such as birth control and ever-rising taxes to support ever expanding government programs. And this has often resulted in both parents working outside the home—not by personal choice but because of economic necessity.

In a recent article in *The Atlantic,* Derek Thompson writes, "The implications of permanently slumped population growth are wide-ranging. Shrinking populations produce stagnant economies. . . . Whether by accident, design, or a total misunderstanding of basic economics, America has steered itself into the demographic danger zone."[22]

But perhaps the biggest factor is faith, with fewer than 50 percent of Americans identifying themselves with any sort of faith background. It is not a coincidence the drop in the birthrate has coincided with the falloff in religious faith. Why? Because religious faith has always resulted in larger families because faith communities see children as a blessing, instead of an inconvenience to achieving one's "self-fulfillment"—a fulfillment that used to come from God and not man.

And with faith comes commitment to marriage and family. A Harvard School of Public Health study found couples who regularly attend church services are about 30–50 percent less likely to divorce.[23]

As faith diminishes, the family is one of the first institutions to suffer. In 1970, there were nearly seventy-seven marriages for every one hundred women fifteen years of age or older. By 2015, that number decreased to thirty-two marriages per one hundred—the lowest rate in American history.[24]

The U.S. Census Bureau recently reported the number of children living with two parents has dropped since 1968, while the percentage living with their mother only has doubled. In 1968, 85 percent of children under eighteen lived with two parents (regardless of marital status); by 2020, 70 percent did.[25]

Thus, what the '60s has wrought for society is this: fewer children who grow up in intact homes; women and children more dependent upon government subsidies to survive; and men who can evade responsibility, and never grow up. All of which is a toxic brew for the long-term survival of a society.

The result is what Robert Rector of the Heritage Foundation has described as a "caste society."[26] Children who grow up in stable homes with two parents end up with all the resulting advantages—a good education and a solid economic base to launch from as they enter adulthood. In contrast, there is a bottom half raised by single parents whose education ends at a high school degree or earlier, and thus, have the door of opportunity slammed directly in their faces.

As Myron Magnet writes, "Time and again, underclass single-parent homes are dysfunctional families. However hard it is for anyone to bring up children without a mate, it can be almost hopelessly so for underclass women . . . many underclass children, already deprived of a father, also suffer bad mothering from harried, ignorant, poor, and sometimes drug dependent women."[27]

He continues, "The mothers of underclass children are as far removed from the mainstream world of work and citizenship as the fathers are. Their alternative of choice is not crime but dependency. Most of them live on Aid to Families with Dependent Children, the nation's principal welfare system."[28]

NO-FAULT DIVORCE

Ronald Reagan called his signing of California's "no-fault divorce" bill in 1969 the greatest mistake he made in public office.[29] Signed with the intent of eliminating the need for couples to fabricate spousal wrongdoing in pursuit of a divorce, it, along with subsequent laws passed in other states, instead opened the floodgates for the dissolution of marriages across the country.

W. Bradford Wilcox of the Institute for Family Studies has written that from 1960 to 1980, the divorce rate more than doubled—from 9.2 divorces per 1,000 married women to 22.6 divorces per 1,000 married women. In addition, approximately half of the children born to married parents in the 1970s saw their parents' divorce, compared to only 11 percent of those born in the 1950s.[30]

He writes, "The nearly universal introduction of no-fault divorce helped to open the floodgates, especially because these laws facilitated unilateral divorce and lent moral legitimacy to the dissolution of marriages."[31]

Like so many other things presented as a "social good" by progressives, no-fault divorce turned out to be the exact opposite. Wilcox writes,

> Proponents of easy divorce argued that the ready availability of divorce would boost the quality of married life, as abused, unfulfilled, or otherwise unhappy spouses were allowed to leave their marriages. Had they been correct, we would expect to see that Americans' reports of marital quality had improved during and after the 1970s. Instead, marital quality fell during the '70s and early '80s. In the early 1970s, 70% of married men and 67% of married women reported being very happy in their marriages; by the early '80s, these figures had fallen to 63% for men and 62% for women. So marital quality dropped even as divorce rates were reaching record highs.[32]

And of course, children were the victims. Sociologist Paul Amato has estimated that if current-day children experienced the same family stability in place in 1960, there would be 750,000 fewer children repeating grades, 1.2 million fewer school suspensions, approximately 500,000 fewer acts of teenage violence, 600,000 fewer kids receiving therapy, and 70,000 fewer suicide attempts annually.[33]

In addition, children of divorce are more likely to approve of and engage in premarital sex, cohabitation, or eventually get divorced themselves.[34] Girls whose fathers left the house before they were five years old are eight times more likely to become pregnant as teenagers than girls from intact homes.[35] Children of divorced parents are also less likely to see marriage as a lifelong commitment and are more likely to cohabitate.[36]

Thus, no-fault divorce, introduced in the late 1960s, has now negatively impacted every future generation, creating cycles of cohabitation, unwed pregnancies, and devastated children.

And along with divorce, comes another impact of the 1960s: the increase in loneliness. For example, the percentage of adults living with a spouse decreased from 52 to 50 percent over the past decade, while the number of adults over the age of eighteen living alone increased to 37 million, up from 33 million in 2011—28 percent of all U.S. households.[37]

The statistics get even more sobering: the estimated median age to marry is now 30.4 years of age for men and 28.6 for women, up from 23.7 and 20.5 in 1947,[38] and 17 percent of men and women between the ages of 25–34 lived with an unmarried partner.[39] Another survey done last year by the wedding website, The Knot, found the average of men and women getting married is now 32 and 30 respectively.[40] And finally, another study found 25 percent of adults over the age of 40 have never been married.[41]

That is just the marriage statistics. For the family, it becomes even more alarming. The number of families with children under the age of eighteen living at home has declined from 48 percent in 2001 to just 40 percent in 2021.[42] The actual share of the 130 million American households, headed by married parents, with children decreased from 18.6 percent in 2020 to 17.8 percent in 2021.[43] In contrast, more than 40 percent of homes in 1970 were headed by married parents with children.[44]

These numbers have all sorts of alarming consequences, not just for individuals, but for society.

First, families provide vital social connections—a husband with his wife, parents with their children, parents with other parents, children with other children—we all need to thrive. These relationships build upon each other, with the family serving as the foundation.

When people live alone, they often lack those connections, leading to loneliness, which can be deadly. In his book, *Loneliness*, University of Chicago professor John Cacioppo wrote about the negative health risks of living alone are far worse than air pollution or obesity.[45]

By systematically weakening the family through making it easier for couples to no longer honor their commitment to each other, we are now a lonelier, less healthy, and more dysfunctional society.

WHERE HAVE ALL THE MEN GONE?

As we have seen, the weakening of the family, starting in the 1960s, has had devastating effects on men and women. For men, many are now adrift, with no male role models to follow and emulate on how to become mature men, good husbands, and loving fathers. For women, this has meant an ever-diminishing pool of "marriable" men.

As a society, we are seeing increasing numbers of boys and young men "fail to launch" into adulthood, seem directionless and unwilling to accept personal responsibility, engage in violent acts, and fall into increasing despair, resulting in major societal problems such as the current opioid crisis, which I will discuss in a bit.

All these are symptoms of a great problem whose root cause is the loss of male identity. This loss has occurred because of the lack of male role models for young men to learn from on how to be a gentleman who puts the needs of others above their own.

For instance, thanks in part to the breakdown of the family over the past fifty-plus years, we now have at least two generations of men who did not have fathers, or other significant male figures in their lives to mentor them and guide them on the right path to be a loving husband, father, and contributor to the common good of society.

Without these positive influences, men can often become angry, despondent, and self-absorbed—all traits not good for them, women, children, and our culture. They become the antithesis of being a gentleman—men who respect women, love children, and take their role as a provider, nurturer, and protector of their family seriously.

As a result, many women in their twenties become increasingly frustrated with the inability to find men worthy of marriage—men who will be professionally successful, loving husbands, and responsible fathers. With a smaller pool to select from, they are not marrying until they are thirty, or not at all.

This is another tragic result of the 1960s. First, the advent of the pill, and then legalization of abortion, gave men a blank check to engage in procreation without having to accept responsibility. Second, government programs removed the need for a man to be financially responsible for the children he fathered, and as discussed earlier, in many ways *encouraged* him not be responsible. Third, the coarsening of entertainment as well as the pornography culture, encouraged men to no longer view women as someone to love and cherish, but instead to use and exploit for purely carnal purposes. Finally, men who took caring financially and emotionally for their wives and families, were told they were blocking the path to "equality" for women, and they needed to get out of the way.

As our society has increased opportunities for women (a very good thing which I affirm wholeheartedly), it has over-compensated for its previous mistreatment by, in many cases, taking opportunities away from men—resulting in an increasing number of perpetual male adolescents who "fail to launch" into adulthood, seem directionless, and unwilling to accept personal responsibility, and fall into increasing despair.

Thus, the culmination of all the items I have listed, most of which came to fruition in the 1960s, has led to the current male regression in society—with women lacking husbands, children lacking fathers, and men becoming increasingly bitter about their state in life.

As a result, these men are "dropping out." For example, nearly 60 percent of college and university students are women. In just over half a century, the pendulum has swung wildly in the female direction, as the percentages were almost exactly reversed in 1969.[46]

In fact, over the past ten years, spring enrollment for men has fallen by more than 18 percent and while total enrollment has been declining for years, men comprised 71 percent of the decline.[47]

So, is it any wonder where all the men have gone? Given society has encouraged male irresponsibility and fueled men's worst instincts, we now face several generations of men who have no idea of the basic concept of "being a man" or even more importantly "being a gentleman." Many of these men have turned to drugs and alcohol, fueling even more societal problems.

Prior to the 1960s, men were perceived as providers, a role most (but not all) men took seriously and our society affirmed. Once that dynamic shifted, it created a cultural earthquake whose damage has now affected generations of men, women, and children, all which are facing various aspects of loss in tragic ways.

THE DRUG CULTURE

The problems for society go beyond "all the lonely people" the Beatles once sang about in their song "Eleanor Rigby." Robert Rector of the Heritage Foundation has written about how the breakdown of marriage and family that started in the 1960s affects our nation's social capital because children in single-parent households are more likely to engage in substance abuse than those in stable, two-parent homes.[48] As mentioned earlier, our nation has seen that play out in the rise of opioid abuse and other drugs—which now have generational impacts.

These children eventually grow into adults and bring their drug dependencies with them, creating another generation of children trapped in the cycle of family dysfunction and drug abuse. It is a triple whammy resulting in a continuing downward spiral of despair and loss of social capital with each succeeding generation. It also creates a two-caste society—those who are healthy and nurtured in a two-parent home versus those who lack an essential parent right from the start.

But as has been said, those who do not know history are doomed to repeat it. As mentioned earlier, we are now seeing the expansion and legalization of the 1960s drug culture (marijuana legalization and so-called "magic mushroom" legalization) specifically targeted at teenage audiences. The same leftists who decried the "candy cigarettes" of the 1960s, which were nothing more than pure sugar, now either turn a blind eye or make a profit from marijuana candy targeted at children and teenagers today.

Meanwhile, just as studies started to come out in the early 1960s about the deadly effects of smoking cigarettes, studies are now beginning to emerge about the mental and physical damage of marijuana and other psychedelic drugs on teenagers today. But thanks to the mindset of the 1960s, these drugs have become socially acceptable regardless of the mounting evidence of their long-term negative's effects on children and society, such as addiction, homelessness, mental illness, and impaired driving.

And ultimately, it is future generations who pay the price for a drug-dependent society putting children at a physical, mental, and financial disadvantage before they even exit the womb.

Another factor in the breakdown of the family and other social pathologies is the drug culture that emerged from the hippie movement. Just as the sexual revolution and mis-guided government programs led to ever-increasing num-bers of single parent families, the drug culture led to young adults becoming hooked on illegal substances, not only negatively impacting them but generations to come.

A classic example of how the policies of the 1960s have led to some astoundingly illogical and dangerous policies in the 2020s, politicians now openly promote the legaliza-tion of drugs, particularly marijuana, so they can tax the revenue to pay for the very programs out-of-control drug abuse created in the first place! It boggles the mind. We are creating new generations of addicts to pay for the problems caused by the previous generation of addicts. It is a deadly cycle.

As with so many other pathologies, a slippery slope emerged in the 1960s. Marijuana led to LSD which led to heroin which led to all sorts of other illegal drugs. Now that same slope has led to the opioid crisis currently facing our nation.

Between 2004 and 2013, the number of babies, accord-ing to the *New York Times*, born with drug dependencies because of their mother's addiction rose nearly seven-fold in rural areas and four-fold in urban areas.[49] Opioids are to blame, and fifteen out of every one hundred babies born in poorer areas are born addicted. This has been especially true in two states, Kentucky and West Virginia, which have seen marriage rates drop by more than 25 percent over the last five decades.[50]

While there are other factors at play, such as the loss of blue-collar jobs and rising poverty, there can be no doubt the decline of marriage which started in the 1960s, coupled with the drug culture emerging during the same decade, have been major factors in fueling the opioid crisis.

And thanks to the legacy of the 1960s, more children are born into addiction and despair with each passing generation.

Opioid-addicted babies face tremendous hardship immediately after exiting their mother's womb. As soon as the umbilical cord is removed, these babies go through withdrawal, which has been described by former addicts as "living in hell." These newborns, having just entered the world minutes earlier, experience vomiting, tremors, and violent temperature changes—all of which cause significant physical and mental damage. In fact, these children will likely experience higher rates of emotional disturbance, anxiety, depression, learning disabilities, and developmental challenges. They are also more likely to become drug users later in life—keeping the cycle going for another generation.

What has happened to these children, and their children, is a tragic example of what the values, or lack of values, of the 1960s have created. And as we will see, the 1960s were, in many ways, the end of childhood in America as children were not only thrust into an adult world long before they were ready but became seen as useful pawns to satisfy adults' selfish desires.

THE END OF INNOCENCE

During the 1960s, the relative innocence of childhood, as described in the letters to a pen pal, died. Liberalized divorce laws, along with the Great Society programs, resulted in children increasingly being raised in single-parent homes, without the vital presence of both parents, in most instances, the father being absent. Thus, the end of the family also results in the end of childhood, as many of us have known it.

Divorce and absent fathers created trauma for boys and girls. For boys, this trauma often manifested itself through aggressive, angry behavior, and lack of focus or motivation. For girls, it led to increased sexual promiscuity and inability to commit to relationships, while also greater difficulty in finding a suitable mate to begin with.

Then to throw gasoline on the fire, our society became increasingly sexualized, (thanks to the Kinsey Report mentioned earlier) particularly with regard to children, exposing and enticing them with explicit sexual messages and material that has only gotten worse with the introduction of the internet. Sexual purity was mocked while sexual "experimentation" was seen as the ideal. The result? Rising teen pregnancies, poverty, increased violence against children, fatherless homes, disrespect for authority, and escalating sexual deviancy.

The emerging drug culture, which started on college campuses in the 1960s, targeted children, particularly those in working class homes, resulting in them making increasingly bad choices that in some cases, led to the end of their lives. And if they survived, they carried the negative consequences of addiction with them for the remainder of their days. As we discussed previously, much of our current homeless and permanent underclass problems can be traced to the ethos of the 1960s.

The nation's educational system, as discussed earlier, no longer taught children the basic life skills they needed to survive and thrive. It also no longer instilled optimism and hope. Instead, it served as a breeding ground for cynicism, guilt, distrust, and despondency.

On top of all this, leftist activists saw children as the gateway to achieving their agenda—just as John Dewey hoped. Thus, children were treated like guinea pigs—often without their parents' permission or knowledge—for every leftist social experiment and indoctrination. This indoctrination has now created a generation of adults who can no longer think for themselves, but instead do what others say and think as they are told—making our society ripe for demagogues. But once again, this is in alignment with the goals of Dewey and Alinsky.

This educational shift, which occurred in the 1960s, has led to the teaching of "gender fluidity" to kindergartners, explicit sex education, access to abortion without parental consent, and other practices with no rational reason to be part of any child's formative years, yet they are, thanks to the 1960s.

The result? Catholic theologian Deborah Savage puts it sadly, "[America's youth] have been left alone in the cosmos with nothing to guide them, not even a firm grasp of what constitutes their basic humanity, and no means of finding the way home."[51]

ENDING LIFE BEFORE IT STARTS

The greatest attack on children is denying them the right to even exist. It was during the 1960s when abortion advocates ramped up their efforts to legalize abortion nationwide, ultimately culminating in the 1973 *Roe v. Wade* decision that played a vital role in claiming more than 60 million innocent lives until it was struck down by the U.S. Supreme Court in 2022.

The Left's crusade against the right to life for preborn children cheapened the intrinsic value of *all* human life as it drastically shifted American society from one that embraced the Judeo-Christian ethic that all life is created in the image of God (*Imago Dei*) and worthy of dignity and respect, to a view that all life is disposable if it is deemed to be inconvenient.

As with so many of the arguments underpinning radical societal changes, the pro-abortion movement achieved success through manipulation and deceit.

One of the key players in their effort was Harriet Pilpel, a lawyer who was a devoted proponent of birth control and population control.[52] Pilpel testified that restricting abortion placed an enormous economic burden on the nation—an argument designed to sway fiscal conservatives to join with leftists to rationalize the killing of preborn children for the "greater good" of society.

Working with groups such as the American Civil Liberties Union (ACLU), Pilpel used highly inflated, and downright dishonest, numbers to make her point. In 1965, she wrote that there were between one and one and a half million abortions in the United States and more than 8,000 maternal deaths from those abortions each year.[53] Her numbers were only off by about one million as later research documented. The truth was, in the early sixties, the number of abortions was closer to 200,000 and there were only 197 abortion-related maternal deaths.[54] This means she exaggerated the number of maternal deaths by a staggering 700 percent!

The ACLU continued to make economic arguments to rationalize its support for abortion. An ACLU fundraising letter actually suggested financially motivated abortions for the poor were far less expensive than paying for childbirth and welfare support—a rather Machiavellian way to justify its actions if there ever was one. In other words, the argument was good financial stewardship meant allowing the government to pay for the killing of preborn children, rather than paying for their upbringing.

But as we saw in previous chapters, this argument falls apart once you analyze the logic behind it. It was the radical attacks on the family and the advancement of the sexual revolution in the 1960s that greatly increased the number of children—particularly at the lower end of the social-economic scale—born out of wedlock or living in other forms of broken families. These attacks, along with the encouragement of "anything goes" sexuality, resulted in greater government dependance and spending.

So, to compound social error upon social error, the progressives of the 1960s devalued the family, trumpeted the very actions leading to greater irresponsibility and dependance, and then offered as its solution the murder of the "perceived problem" (a preborn child) in order to allow themselves to live a life of "spontaneity" without responsibility.

And the true victims of adult irresponsibility are the children who pay the price for being the often-unwanted products of the lauded spontaneity of the 1960s.

CHAPTER EIGHT

The Religious Stumble

In the end, when all else had been leveled, the 1960s went after God.[1]

—Judge J. Harvie Wilkinson III

Relevant Christianity doesn't stay relevant for long. Reinterpreted Christianity may appeal to the deconstructing, but it does not win the hearts and minds of the lost. We have no guarantee that faithful churches will thrive. But after almost 60 years of constant mainline decline, we have a pretty good idea of how churches die.[2]

—Kevin DeYoung

The churches that have tried to protect themselves from intolerance by ceding to its demands are dying. They do not replace themselves literally or figuratively; their morale is low; some will not even exist a hundred years from now. Responding to intolerance with capitulation is like trying to put out a house fire by throwing dynamite at it.[3]

—Mary Eberstadt

While the march toward liberalism immolating mainline Protestant churches started back in the progressive era, much of it, like with our universities, was hatched in the relatively silent liberal takeover of seminaries in the 1950s while America was perhaps at its churchgoing peak.

In the 1960s, nearly every mainline Protestant denomination, but in particular, Church of Christ (Congregationalist), Lutheran, Methodist, Presbyterian, and Episcopalian, and some Catholic churches and institutions discarded belief in the fundamental tenets of the Bible such as biblical inerrancy and that it is only through faith in Jesus Christ that one can obtain eternal life.

In addition, these churches rejected sexual purity, and male-female complementarianism, and embraced radical sexual liberation and the progressive ethos. In addition, these churches started to attack, rather than celebrate, America and our role in the world.

It is no coincidence radical activists sought to take over mainstream religion—where else can you get a captive and trusting audience once a week to convert to your views?

While the 1950s are still looked upon as the height of American spirituality, there were definite storm clouds on the horizon. Yes, record numbers of Americans were going to church, and many still espoused, even if they didn't necessarily adhere to, an established moral code. The mainline religion of the 1950s was socially acceptable, did not require sacrifice, and in many instances, was more therapeutic than challenging. For many, church attendance was simply a box to be checked off each week. In many ways, American spirituality was a mile wide but an inch deep.

Thus, churches focusing more on preaching platitudes than on genuine and authentic faith and discipleship, were ripe for takeover by radical leftists seeking spiritual cover and approval for their secular agendas. By trying to be relevant, as Kevin DeYoung noted, they became irrelevant instead— and in the process enabled the acceleration of moral and cultural decay while losing fans quicker than a 100-loss baseball team.[4]

In his book *The Fractured Republic,* Yuval Levin writes:

> These churches reached their peak in the 1950s, when the nation's core institutions were still strong and firm. . . . But like other core American institutions of the period, these churches were already being transformed from within just as they reached their apex of power. Where they might have been expected to act as restraints on the excesses of a liberalizing culture, the mainline churches in particular, chose instead to become an accelerant, adopting every fashionable trend and excusing every countercultural tendency of the 1960s. In essence, they were undermining their own authority while they undermined trust in the nation's elite institutions.[5]

After the 1960s, conservative churches became the remnant instead of the "mainstream," with the outlier churches now seen as threats to society rather than stabilizing forces.

Yet, while mainstream denominations were bleeding members, conservative evangelical churches, the new counterculture in Christianity, were growing. But because of the mainline denomination's embrace of liberalism in the 1960s, there is no longer a clear and consistent message of Christ from our churches. Instead, America increasingly hears a confused and muddled voice when it comes to matters of faith.

This has also resulted in the weakening of Christian witness and in providing cover for the full societal implementation of the progressive sexual agenda—including abortion, the redefinition of marriage, gender identity, and leftist economic theory—through organized religion.

And without that clear voice, Americans tuned religion out. The mainline Protestant congregations have now become increasingly irrelevant, living off endowments and with aging populations who attend more out of tradition than a vibrant, growing faith, slowly dying off and leaving nothing but empty pews and decaying buildings. In fact, increasing numbers of churches—as seen by the numbers of closing PCUSA, United Methodists, United Church of Christ, and Evangelical Lutherans churches—are shutting their doors at an alarming rate.

In the 1960s, religion, but particularly Protestantism and Catholicism, came under attack, particularly via the sexual revolution. Some churches stood firm to support traditional teachings regarding human sexuality, while, as I have mentioned, those embracing this new "liberation" started to fade. This threw open the door for other religions besides Christianity to gain a foothold, and starting in Northern California, groups such as transcendental meditation, Buddhism, Hare Krishnas, Satanism, Scientology, and EST gained attention.[6]

As Yuval Levin writes:

> That loss of faith had direct consequences for the strength of the churches themselves. Membership in the Lutheran, United Methodist, Episcopalian, and Presbyterian churches all peaked in the late 1960s and began a sharp decline. American Catholicism went into a tailspin too; although the church's overall membership remained steady (thanks to the rising Catholic immigration from Latin America), its institutions fell into a deep crisis in the 1970s as Mass attendance and religious vocations plummeted.[7]

Or as Judge J. Harvie Wilkinson III puts it, "Americans have always been a religious people, and in many ways, we still are. But I suspect we are fewer religious people as a result of living through the 1960s."[8]

On a positive note, the 1960s separated the "wheat from the chaff" between those who were truly committed to the faith and those "playing church." But on a negative note, with a weaker and less authoritative voice, the American church lost its ability to be "salt and light" by choosing to blend into the increasingly coarsening culture.

"OPEN MINDS," EMPTY PEWS, CLOSING DOORS

A 2020 study by Lifeway Research, affiliated with the Southern Baptist Convention, found that in 2019—before the COVID-19 pandemic which would only accelerate the decline in church attendance—4,500 Protestant churches closed in comparison to 3,000 new ones opening. Just five years earlier, in 2014, 4,000 churches opened, compared to 3,700 closing.[9]

A study done by the Center for Analytics, Research, and Data, which is affiliated with the liberal United Church of Christ, was even more alarming. It found for the decade ending in 2020, houses of worship closed at the rate of 75–100 congregations *per week*—with an estimated 3,850–7,700 churches closing per year.[10] Another poll by Gallup found church/synagogue/mosque membership declined from 70 to 47 percent of the population in the period from 2000 to 2020.[11]

The biggest decline has been in the denominations that discarded biblical truth in the 1960s. At their peak in 1965, mainline Protestant churches counted 31 million members out of a U.S. population of fewer than 200 million.[12] But then the great decline started and remains unabated to this day. Ten years later, nearly a third of Americans were still affiliated with mainline denominations. But now, just one in ten Americans are.[13] The Presbyterian Church USA (PCUSA) had four million members sixty years ago. It has 1.2 million now.[14]

While the following statistics from the Gospel Coalition are a decade old (2012–2015), they illustrate the drastic shrinking of mainline denominational churches (which have shrunk even further since, as noted in the PCUSA numbers):

Christian Church (Disciples of Christ)
1965: 1,918,471 members
2012: 625,252 members (67 percent decline)

Reformed Church in America
1967: 384,751 members
2014: 145,466 members (62 percent decline)

United Church of Christ (Congregationalist)
1965: 2,070,413 members
2012: 998,906 members (52 percent decline)

Episcopal Church
1966: 3,647,297 members
2013: 1,866,758 members (49 percent decline)

Presbyterian Church U.S.A. (PCUSA)
1967: 3,304,321 members
2013: 1,760,200 members (47 percent decline)
—now 1.2 million

United Methodist Church
1967: 11,206,976 members
2012: 7,391,911 members (33 percent decline)[15]

As stated earlier, this is overwhelming evidence Americans are tuning out the denominations that served as the religious backbone of the nation for decades.

The downward trend in religious faith in America, particularly among the old mainline denominations, started to occur when they drifted away from preaching truth to embrace "social justice." Without absolute truth as an anchor to fortify one's faith, the church became nothing more than another philanthropic group or social club of like-minded adherents without a compelling reason to be a member.

What each of these declining denominations have in common is this adoption of the sexual and cultural ethos of the 1960s. As each denomination, and the churches within them, moved to the Left, they lost members and relevance.

What is interesting is the churches that continued to preach biblical truth continued to grow during the same time period:

Church of God in Christ
1965: 425,000 members
2012: 5,499,875 (1,194 percent increase)

Presbyterian Church in America (founded in the early '70s as a conservative alternative to the PCUSA)
1973: 41,232 members
2013: 367,033 members (790 percent increase)

Evangelical Free Church of America
1965: 43,851 members
2013: 372,321 members (749 percent increase)

Assemblies of God
1965: 572,123 members
2013: 3,030,944 members (430 percent increase)

African Methodist Episcopal Church
1951: 1,166,301 members
2012: 2,500,000 members (114 percent increase)

Southern Baptist Convention
1965: 10,770,563 members
2013: 15,735,640 members (46 percent increase)[16]

Looking at these numbers, there can be no denying the denominations that abandoned the Bible and absolute truth are going the way of the horse and buggy and the dodo bird, while those that have stayed true to Scripture have continued to grow.

Thus, while those on the Left decry what they perceive to be the politicalization of the church by conservatives, it is the Left's actual politicalization of our churches in the 1960s that led to the decline of so many denominations.

INCREASING IRRELEVANCY

But the decline of the mainline denominations did change the way many Americans perceive religion. As former *New York Times* columnist Ross Douthat wrote, the result was a movement "away from institutional religion and toward a more do-it-yourself and consumer-oriented spirituality—that endures to this day."[17]

With weakened familial or traditional ties to mainline denominations, Americans have turned into a society of church shoppers whose loyalty is often up for sale to the highest bidder. It has also led to increased individualism—i.e., the "lone wolf" Christian, who still professes faith, but is not part of any church body at all.

The other movement, as the mainline denominations abandoned biblical truth, was toward "alternative religions" that are not Christian at all in faith and tradition. Levin writes,

> Many have ceased to view religious traditionalism as an ideal with which to nominally identify and have come to see it as an option to reject. This is not a

minor shift. It is in fact a kind of revolution in the structure of American religiosity; formerly loosely affiliated members of the traditional streams of Christianity are drifting away and a broader array of softer and thinner religious and spiritual views are emerging. It has also, without doubt, involved more Americans becoming hostile to religion to varying degrees.[18]

Levin concludes this has resulted in social and religious conservatives losing their place of honor in society and finding themselves in a place of scorn as Americans abandon the biblical truths mainline denominations used to stand for. He states, "[They] have increasingly found themselves locked into conflict with social liberals who present themselves as rejecting all moral judgementalism, but who in fact, unavoidably, end up trying to judge society by a new standard instead."[19]

The abandonment of biblical truth in churches since the 1960s has not only led to a hemorrhaging of members but also increasing numbers of youth who have become alienated from the faith. Because these churches are no longer salt and light in their communities, they have become increasingly irrelevant. By conforming to the culture, rather than transforming it, they are rapidly disappearing from the culture completely.

In response, rather than go to church, many young people left the church and never came back. Conservative youth were repelled by the liberal church's growing abandonment of the Bible, and leftist youth felt the church was too passive and not aggressive enough in pursuing a progressive agenda. By trying to be "relevant," the church became increasingly irrelevant, and thus rejected by both sides of the aisle.

Ironically, if young people did come back to faith, it was through conservative churches, such as the Calvary

Chapel movement of the early 1970s as documented in the 2023 movie *Jesus Revolution*. Such restoration of faith was not achieved by liberal churches abandoning historical teachings.

Unsurprisingly, the young revolutionaries who wrote the *Port Huron Statement*, and their followers today, lump the church in with government, big business, and the military as components of "the Establishment"—and as such, in the words of Joanne Beckman from Duke University, was ripe for attack because of perceived materialism, internal politics, hypocrisy, and complacency.[20]

Sadly, the same voices that led to the church's abandonment of truth and subsequent decline are calling for the church to repeat this mistake and forsake truth to reach younger generations. These voices are recommending the church embrace a bevy of trendy social issues and concerns to entice young churchgoers.

Yet true social justice only occurs from a citizenry that embraces the truth of Scripture—in particular that we are all made *Imago Dei*, in the image of God, and thus all human beings should be treated with dignity and respect. The "social justice" drift of the past sixty years has only left empty pews, often with a few gray-haired individuals scattered across an increasingly cavernous sanctuary.

For instance, according to a 2022 Pew Research Study, 73 percent of adults between the ages of thirty to thirty-four (millennials born in the 1980s and early 1990s) now have no religious affiliation. The number in that age range raised in homes identifying as Christian dropped from 90 percent in 1990 to 65 percent in 2020.[21]

Another study done by the American National Family Life Survey in December 2021, found Generation Z (born between the late 1990s-early 2010s) are also far more likely to identify as atheist or agnostic. Eighteen percent of Gen Z affirmatively identifies as either atheist (9 percent) or agnostic (9 percent). In contrast, fewer than one in ten (9 percent) of Baby Boomers and 4 percent of the Silent Generation identifies as atheist or agnostic.[22]

In response to these alarming numbers, many churches have resorted to gimmicks or social justice crusades instead of truth to get youth back through their doors.

Over the past sixty years, churches have poured millions of dollars into youth programs emphasizing entertainment and marketing over truth. The result is many young people walked away because they saw no difference between the church and the world, or because they had no biblical foundation the minute their faith was challenged, or simply because they faced temptations they were not equipped to combat. It is ironic that we have probably spent more money on youth ministry than ever before, and we are still seeing more and more youth walk away from the faith. Kids want boundaries and truth, in the home and at church. When neither provides them, they end up shunning both institutions.

Thus, when parents and churches abdicate their roles in raising children in the faith, and I mean by that, in biblical truth, it is no wonder these kids become agnostic, atheist, or indifferent when worldly forces swoop in.

THE ABANDOMENT OF BIBLICAL SEXUALITY

In addition, as our society has de-buckled itself from the institution of marriage, with catastrophic results, and the church, as mainline denominations did in the 1960s, abandons biblical principles on human sexuality, the line between the church and greater society as a whole becomes increasingly blurred.

As the church chooses to conform to the culture rather than transforming it, its voice in our culture becomes weaker—to the point of irrelevance—and our children are paying the price. This is evident in the following statistics, especially when it comes to today's young adults—even those in what are perceived to be conservative, evangelical churches.

A few years ago, Pew Research reported 58 percent of white evangelicals said cohabitation was acceptable as long as the couple eventually plans to marry.[23] Alarming as that statistic is, it is more sobering among young evangelicals. Nine years ago, a General Social Survey reported more than 40 percent of evangelicals between the ages of twenty and twenty-nine thought cohabitation was acceptable even if they had *no* plans to marry.[24]

Another survey from David Ayers at the Institute of Family Studies finds nearly half of evangelical Protestants between the ages of fifteen to twenty-two who are not presently cohabitating or married believe they will likely cohabit with a member of the opposite sex sometime in the future.[25]

The study also found 65 percent of evangelicals between the ages of twenty-three and forty-four who had already cohabitated plan on doing so again. This will not only impact the church's witness with regard to marriage and family, but also accelerate the continued fragmentation of the family unit—the stabilizing factor in all civilizations—regardless of faith.

It sounds like the teachings of Herbert Marcuse and Alfred Kinsey have been the focus of Sunday sermons instead of Jesus Christ.

Why has this happened? In the rush to be seen as "culturally relevant," "tolerant," and "non-judgmental," many Christians and churches have pushed aside biblical teachings regarding marriage and family. While there is obviously nothing wrong with churches trying to reach the unchurched, many have chosen to avoid so-called "hot topics"—especially when it comes to human sexuality—leaving a vacuum our culture is eager to fill.

A generation of young believers is learning more about sex and marriage from popular culture rather than from their churches. When the world, and not the church, is the main educator on these issues, the results are dismal.

HOPE

But there is hope. While public opinion polls share what seem to be depressing statistics about the religiosity of young Americans, those polls only share numbers, not commitment.

Many Bible-believing churches that have opened their doors have found young adults flocking inside—drawn to authentic faith, instead of the "going through the motions" faith of the churches that abandoned biblical truths in the 1960s. They are also rejecting the evangelical overcorrection to "be relevant" by watering down messages or trying to conform, rather than transform the culture.

And despite how hard progressives have worked to stamp out religion, it keeps on coming back, especially as young adults mature.

David Keene wrote in *The Washington Times*:

> The common wisdom these days is that younger people increasingly skeptical about both organized churches and religion itself will carry that into their later years, leading to a steady decline in church attendance and the number of Americans who consider religion important. That however has been called into question by recent studies . . . demonstrating that as young people age, they become increasingly religious.[26]

A good friend of mine and his wife who live in a large metropolitan area launched a young adult ministry about four years ago—deciding to open their house to any young adult who wished to come and experience serious Bible discussion and authentic community. That small group eventually led to the church becoming aware of the need to reach young adults between the ages of twenty and thirty-five and starting a Tuesday night young adults' group. That group now draws well over one hundred young adults each week, many of whom drive from over fifty miles away, because they are hungry for biblical truth.

That is how we are going to reverse the 1960s' damage to religion—not by trying to out-social justice each other or water down truth to make it "palatable," but by opening our doors and hearts to future generations—who, once they hear the real gospel will respond and reject the false gospel of the 1960s.

CHAPTER NINE

The Civility Stumble

*The Sixties encouraged us to fight such domestic differences
to the death, to square off in opposing camps and armies,
to slay the religious right as zealots or the secular left as
infidels. We strike our mutual blows as though our nation
was exempt from history's laws and reckonings, as though
it wouldn't even matter what one day happens from
abroad so long as enemies at home are suitably debased.*[1]
—Judge J. Harvie Wilkinson III

*The most flamboyantly anti-American rhetoric of 60s
radicals are now more or less conventional wisdom among
many progressives: America, the land of white supremacy
and structural racism and patriarchy, the perpetrator of
indigenous displacement and genocide, the world's biggest
polluter, and so on.*[2]
—Brink Lindsey

In 2022, Gallup asked Americans if they were proud of
their country. Sadly, a record low of only 38 percent said
they were proud to be an American, with only 27 percent
saying they were very proud.[3]

Other polls have shown a decreasing number of young
people who are willing to fight for our country.[4] Meanwhile,

progressives have made a hero/martyr out of individuals such as former pro quarterback Colin Kaepernick, who has made a fortune disrespecting the American flag and our country. Baseball players who refused to kneel, as did Kaepernick, as our National Anthem played during the 2020 season were vilified on social media by so-called tolerant progressives.

Right became wrong, and wrong became right. But it was all a culmination of the disrespect for America and its institutions that started in the late 1960s.

In 1967, then-Governor of California Ronald Reagan said in his gubernatorial inaugural address, "Freedom is a fragile thing, and it's never more than one generation away from extinction. It is not ours by way of inheritance; it must be fought for and defended constantly by each generation, for it comes only once to a people. And those in world history who have known freedom and then lost it have never known it again."[5]

Unfortunately, given the current state of American patriotism and duty to country, his comments have proven to be prophetic. We are losing our freedom because we no longer have an appreciation for it. Like a trust fund baby who gets money he or she never earned, we not only lack gratitude for the sacrifices made to create that fortune, but we end up looking back with disdain at those who bequeathed it to us in the first place.

Sadly, all this has taken a terrific toll, especially on our youth. The Gallup poll which I mentioned at the beginning of the chapter found only 18 **percent** of eighteen to thirty-four-year-olds say they are proud to be an American. Forty-six percent of the same group now view capitalism negatively.[6]

Ingrid Jacques commented, "We can't blame young people for not loving and defending a system they don't understand and one they've been taught is deeply flawed in many ways."[7]

Our current lack of patriotism can be directly traced to the 1960s when traditional values, the military, and respect for all authority came under attack by progressives—the "trust fund babies" who came after the generation that survived the Great Depression, fought World War II, and then worked hard and built wealth in the 1950s.

In fact, the genesis of Colin Kaepernick's protest can be traced back to 1968 and the Mexico City Olympics when two runners, Tommy Smith and John Carlos, gave the "black power" salute while standing on the podium receiving their medals. Unlike Kaepernick who quickly became a hero of the far Left and reaped millions of dollars in endorsements from corporations such as Nike, Smith and Carlos were widely criticized, sent home packing, and faded into relative obscurity, only to be remembered by the Left in wake of the "Black Lives Matter" movement of 2020–2021.[8]

Now to be fair, there was still great prejudice toward black Americans at the time of Smith's and Carlos's protest. But their protest was just another manifestation of the 1960s mindset that downright disrespect, and in some cases violence, was justified to achieve one's ends, rather than rational discourse.

Their protest was upsetting because in 1968, despite the tumult going on around them, the majority of Americans were patriotic. They supported the troops in Vietnam, they saluted the flag, they stood for "The Star-Spangled Banner." When the nation witnessed the 1968 riots at the Democratic National Convention in Chicago by anti-war, anti-America protestors, along with the burning of the American flag in cities across the country, many recoiled in horror—and voted for Richard Nixon and his "law and order" platform. They were the core of what Nixon called the "silent majority."

But to quote Saul Alinsky, If you push a negative hard and deep enough it will break through into its counterside; this is based on the principle that every positive has its negative."

That is what the vocal minority did and continued to do with various attacks on American institutions—such as religion, the military, and the family. All of this has resulted in decreased national pride, as the Left has tried to shame and vilify anyone or any institution that believes in American exceptionalism. Being a patriot now labels you as an "extremist" who is a danger to our nation's well-being.

To quote the song my pen pal wrote about, we became a nation of hammers, hitting each other over the head in anger over our differences, rather than linking arms and working together for the common good.

A HOUSE DIVIDED

This disrespect has only widened America's divides. We have become a country divided against itself: women vs. men, race vs. race, liberals vs. conservatives, children vs. parents. The list goes on and on. The result is a toxic brew of dangerous chemicals—rights over responsibilities, and entitlements over sacrifice. That brew only needed a match thrown upon it to explode. That match was the internet.

Thomas Carothers and Andrew O'Donohue, authors of the book *Democracies Divided*, state our country's polarization runs particularly deep in the U.S., in part because American polarization is "especially multifaceted." They write about a "powerful alignment of ideology, race, and religion renders America's divisions unusually encompassing and profound. It is hard to find another example of polarization in the world fusing all three major types of identity divisions in a similar way."[9]

More studies prove this out. In 2018, a Public Religion Research Institute (PRRI) poll found 47 percent of Americans believed our nation has changed so much they felt "like a stranger in their own country." Nearly six in ten Republicans felt alienated because of all the changes that have occurred, compared to four in ten Democrats. The PRRI commented on the findings: "The survey finds that partisans see two entirely different American futures."[10]

A June 2018 Rasmussen poll found 31 percent of likely U.S. voters said it was "Likely" the United States would undergo a second civil war in their lifetime, with 11 percent saying it was "Very Likely."[11] Another poll found 80 percent of Americans believe we live in a divided nation.[12]

As Gerald Harlan Reynolds, law professor at the University of Tennessee, warns, "Marriage counselors say that when a couple views one another with contempt, it's a top indicator that the relationship is likely to fail. Americans, who used to know how to disagree with one another without being mutually contemptuous, seem to be forgetting this."[13]

J. Harvie Wilkinson adds:

I thought blue and gray were the last colors to describe the two Americas. But red and blue now seem part of two very different flags. The two Americas embrace divergent narratives. Red America would restore those values that the Sixties stole away; Blue America seeks to protect the Sixties' gains. Red America invokes an idyllic life before the 1960s—when respect for family and parenthood reigned, when religion existed as a guide to larger meaning, and character formed the gateway to a worthy life. . . . What Red America sees as permissiveness; Blue America sees as personal freedom . . .[14]

Up until the 1960s, while they had significant disagreements, liberals and conservatives found ways to put aside their differences to achieve common goals. For instance, Ronald Reagan, who disagreed with the economic policies of Franklin Roosevelt, would often share how highly he thought of Roosevelt's conduct during World War II. When it came to issues of national importance, the Left and Right could unite to achieve a purpose: in this case the defeat of the Axis Powers and the preservation of freedom.

Republicans and Democrats could sit next to each other at a ballgame, in the church pew, or just be good friends, like conservative Jimmy Stewart and liberal Henry Fonda were. One (Stewart) was a dedicated Presbyterian family man who had a forty-four-year-long marriage. The other, Fonda, an agnostic, endured several divorces. They could bicker over politics, but at the end of the day, they remained good and devoted friends who cared deeply about each other despite their differences.

But that unity enabling people with disparate views to remain friends started to unravel in the 1960s, and the toll on our civil discourse and respect for our fellow human beings, regardless of our differences, has been massive. This lack of respect knew no bounds, as children turned against parents, the irreligious attacked the religious, race was pitted against race, and a war was launched between the sexes.

This was the goal of Saul Alinsky, and he achieved it.

When then Secretary of State Dean Rusk attempted to attend a banquet of the Foreign Policy Association in New York, he was nearly pelted by eggs, rocks, and bags of cows' blood by a radical group whose offensive name I will not repeat. While he was able to enter the hotel unscathed, the radical protestors made their point.[15]

Other administration officials were spat upon and called "baby killers" (ironically by the same people who would later advocate for baby-killing via legalized abortion).

Defense Secretary Robert McNamara had his Colorado home almost set on fire twice, and even after he left office someone tried to physically throw him off a ferry at Martha's Vineyard.[16]

Daniel Patrick Moynihan, a Democrat, had his Cambridge, Massachusetts, home threatened by arsonists, and his family had to go underground, with his ten-year-old son fearful his dad would be assassinated.[17]

Flash-forward to 2022 and the assaults on the homes of the Supreme Court justices after the *Dobbs* decision which overturned *Roe v. Wade*, and you can see where this mob violence and lack of respect and decorum started—in the 1960s.

In homes nationwide, children have turned against parents, and parents have turned against children over political matters. I have friends who have not seen their children or grandchildren for years because of this.

In the last few political cycles, commentators on the Left openly called for children to confront, vilify, and humiliate any relatives, including parents, who may have voted for conservatives, at family get-togethers such as Thanksgiving and Christmas. Rather than encouraging people to look beyond politics to find points of commonality, these cultural influencers and their leaders set out to deliberately exacerbate tensions by turning the holidays—times when Americans normally put differences aside to appreciate each other—into a battle royale of angry partisan warfare.

But this is not isolated to the Left. Others on the right speak of those on the Left with equal venom and derision. Instead of respecting each other's differences and trying to find common ground on issues, such as sex trafficking and drug overdoses to name just two, we instead vilify those who oppose us without ever reaching out to them to understand what they believe and why.

Unfortunately, some conservatives have chosen to return fire with fire when faced with ridicule, creating greater division and turning off many who are both patriotic and believe in civility. By using the same tactics utilized by progressives, conservatives have often alienated potential allies.

This is not a surprise. This type of behavior harkens back to Saul Alinsky's rule: "Ridicule is man's most potent weapon." The adoption of Alinsky's rules, written and implemented in the 1960s by the radical left, resulted in a venomous national discourse where both sides seemingly try to out-ridicule the other.

Thus, while ridicule, regardless of which side of the political spectrum engages in it, should be condemned, it usually results in one of two responses: either complete capitulation to the other side or increased defiance and anger from those being attacked. Thus, the zero-sum game we see played out by both sides in our current culture.

As mentioned earlier, the 1960s also ushered in a wave of disrespect for the military. Using the Vietnam War as their launching pad, America's heroes were now depicted by progressives as villains in classrooms and entertainment. Returning veterans, many of whom were wounded in combat or saw their fellow soldiers die, were greeted with taunts and boos, spat upon, and other forms of harassment upon returning to our shores. For many, this resulted in PTSD and other disorders, including drug abuse, and in the most tragic cases, suicide.

It made no sense to attack the soldiers, sailors, airmen, and Marines who were sent to war by those in Washington. It's ironic how some of the ones spitting on our troops returning from Vietnam are now the ones sending our bravest and best around the world to fight and die.

And as I stated in the introduction, American patriotism is at an all-time low. But if you live in a culture and are raised in an educational system that tells you how evil and corrupt your nation is, which was the mindset of the 1960s radicals who drafted the *Port Huron Statement*, why would you be inclined to support it and defend it?

And that is the ultimate goal of the agenda of the progressives like Roger Baldwin, John Dewey, and so many others who sought to transform America into a totally different country than the Founding Fathers intended. And unless we as Americans stand up to take it back, they will ultimately succeed.

But the tide is turning, as I will address in the last chapter.

CHAPTER TEN

Reviving The Dream: The Road Back From The 1960S' Stumble

In certain important cultural respects, America is still living under the sign of Aquarius, however tattered and faded after the eras of hyperinflation and Reagan.[1]

—Myron Magnet

By 1965, the young and progressive American collective consciousness was at once raised, altered, and liberated as experimentation with drugs, protest, and sexuality crashed through cultural barriers. . . . But by the turn of the decade, the utopian dream had imploded.[2]

—Shawn Parr

The 1960s did not end in 1970. They haunt us even now. Many Americans sense the world unraveling around them and wonder why. They want to know why they feel anxious about all that awaits their children and grandchildren. There are many reasons why, but one of the main reasons is the 1960s.[3]

—Judge J. Harvie Wilkinson III

A decade that had begun with dreams of a new society, a great society, where no one was poor or exploited, where everyone would be educated, and where the sins of America's past, like racism, would be redressed, ended with rejection of the liberal agenda of large-scale government intervention, and with liberal activism now blamed for the chaos consuming the country.[4]

—Harvard Sitkoff

We are now living in the seventh decade of what the 1960s has wrought: disrespect for our country, mockery of faith, broken families, aimless and angry males, sexual promiscuity, traumatized and confused youth, catastrophic national debt, and many other social ills.

Our nation has paid a great price for the cultural and societal wreckage the 1960s inflicted, and we are experiencing the negative ramifications of straying from the spiritual and cultural foundations that held firm before that fateful decade.

As we have seen, in the 1960s, America experienced a second revolution: the sexual and moral revolution. It was during this period the American family, which served as the backbone of society, was dismissed as "outmoded" and "patriarchal." Abortion, while always sadly present in our society, went from something seen as a tragedy to something to be celebrated. Sexual relations outside of marriage were trumpeted as the new norm, and virginity became mocked. We forsook the virtues that stabilized our nation for generations, despite the tolerance of other sins such as slavery and racism.

Our Founders rightly warned that we could not have freedom without virtue, but since the 1960s, a large portion of our nation has chosen to forsake virtue for license. The result has been the loss of freedom—religious freedom, free speech, freedom of association—an ever-expanding government, out-of-control federal spending, dysfunctional educational system resulting in diminished economic opportunities, incivility, and the breakdown of the family. Rather than creating utopia, the radical idealists of the 1960s opened a Pandora's box, unleashing innumerable social pathologies upon America. As a nation, we've spent the past sixty years trying to rein in those pathologies, only to see, like cancer, they continue to metastasize and take on new forms.

Judge J. Harvie Wilkinson comments, "In the 1960s, we lost much of the true meaning of education, much of our capacity for lasting personal commitments, much of our appreciation for the rule of law, and much of our sense of rootedness and home. We started to also lose the sense of those things that are larger than ourselves: the desire for service, the feeling for country, the need for God."[5]

Sadly, much of the social upheaval occurred while good people were sleeping—as during the incrementalism of the progressive movement from the turn of the twentieth century until the 1960s, for example—and blissfully unaware of how their country was being hijacked by radicals who slowly infiltrated and took over every avenue of power and influence: schools, churches, academia, entertainment, local governments, and so forth.

If we are to reverse the damage the '60s has caused, our nation will need to undergo a third revolution—one returning it to the spiritual foundation upon which it was built. America will not resolve its current crisis without a restoration of faith and the virtues that come with it.

Thankfully, Americans are finally waking up. They are seeing the cultural decay the 1960s wrought and are taking action to reverse the damage. Parents are seeing their children, who were indoctrinated in our public education system, turn on them and their values, and are finally saying "enough." The school board battles of 2022–2023 are the long-delayed reaction to the leftist takeover of education in the 1960s.

The current backlash against so-called "woke" ideology promoted in all aspects of our culture—including corporate America—is another manifestation of the awakening of Americans to where the 1960s has taken us as a nation.

Others are finally seeing the end game of progressive ideology: homelessness, the elimination of gender differences, and lawlessness, and they are taking a stand. A recent Gallup poll found a sharp rise in the number of Americans who are embracing social conservatism. More Americans (38 percent) today are saying they are very conservative or conservative on social issues than in 2022 (33 percent) and 2021 (30 percent). The percentage saying their social views are very liberal or liberal has dipped to 29 percent from 34 percent over the same time period, while the segment claiming to be moderate on social issues (31 percent) remains basically the same.[6]

Gallup states the increase in a conservative view of social issues over the past two years is seen among nearly all political and demographic subgroups. Republicans increased from 60 percent in 2021 to 74 percent today, while independents had an uptick of five percentage points, from 24 percent to 29 percent. Meanwhile, there was no change among Democrats, who remained at 10 percent.

The greatest increase in social conservatism has been among middle-aged adults, where we see a double-digit increase in conservative social ideology in those between the ages of thirty and sixty-four. There was also a modest increase in conservative social ideology among young adults.[7]

David Keene writes:

Gallup also found a growing fear that the nation is in moral decline. One can sense a coming backlash against the brands, governments, and institutions responsible. There is a distinct possibility that America's traditional values may be far more resistant to the change on which progressives are banking than they believe. Progressives may remain comfortably isolated in their country clubs, elite neighborhoods, and upscale vacation spots to which they retreat to hold political and marketing strategy meetings. But in the real America, the future may be brighter for the conservative values than they think.[8]

This is encouraging news if these individuals transfer their beliefs into action steps. But temporary action will not suffice. Progressives expect short-term pushback from ordinary Americans, but they've witnessed how quickly such objections peter out, allowing progressives to continue aggressively pushing their agenda. The conservative gains of the 1980s, many of which have now been erased, are a perfect example.

That is why this effort requires perseverance. Looking at things like the ever-soaring national debt, family breakdown, a bankrupt public education system, and the cultural rot of modern entertainment, the challenge seems overwhelming.

But we must remember it took the progressives over sixty years to achieve their goal of a radical transformation of America. Thus, those who seek to return America to its founding principles must start by raising new generations of children who have the critical thinking skills to see through the societal and cultural rot thrust upon them.

The cost of not doing anything is too high. If we do nothing, America will continue to drift away from its freedoms, and as Ronald Reagan warned us, we will never see that freedom again. And, as Abraham Lincoln warned us, quoting Jesus, "a house divided against itself cannot stand."

Those of us over forty may not see the complete reversal of the 1960s' excesses during our lifetime. But it is possible our children and grandchildren will if we act now. It is for their sake we must remain engaged in the battle.

Embracing conservative social values is a start, but there is so much more we must do. America tried that step in the 1980s, but when those beliefs did not result in action, the radicals who shaped and implemented the 1960s' agenda continued to move forward fairly unimpeded.

We must show up at school boards to expose and refute 1960s-inspired indoctrination. We must produce alternatives to the current entertainment fare. We must stop voting for personal and financial gain, but instead for our national welfare. We must continue to pledge allegiance to the flag and be good citizens, rather than complain about the state of our nation and demonize those with opposing views.

We must work to build consensus, rather than seek to bludgeon others into submission. Change happens through building bridges, not burning them. That is why while we stand, we must do so with respect for those who do not understand the groups that brought us the 1960s and exploited their power to pursue radical agendas.

As Carl Trueman instructs us, "The task of the Christian is not to whine about the moment in which he or she lives, but to understand its problems and respond appropriately to them."[9] Thus, we must stop whining, and start doing, but always in a way that directs people back to God.

It all starts with us. If we stop the downward slide of our nation started in the 1960s, it means we must engage, not disengage. We need to be positive lights in our communities, rather than just screaming at the darkness. We need to reach out to those whose lives are collateral damage of the 1960s and provide them with a helping hand and hope, rather than condemning them for actions they have no ability to understand because they have grown up in a culture without a moral compass to guide them.

For instance, for those children who are the victims of the sexual revolution, trying to navigate through life without a father or mother to guide them, we can become that person providing them with the direction they need. As men, we can be role models to both young men and women of what it means to be a loving husband and father, so they have a positive example to emulate. For women, they can provide the nurturing and encouraging environment so many children, teens, and young adults have never received. Rather than leaving them exposed to an entertainment world that seeks to devalue life and ridicule all that is good, we can introduce them to entertainment that affirms basic values, such as civility, love for neighbor, sacrifice, and patriotism. And yes, this kind of entertainment can be done with excellence to engage and inspire. Christians bearing the *Imago Dei* energized by the Holy Spirit possess far greater creativity than any demonic force.

I have a dear friend who, "I mentioned earlier," along with his wife, has done all of this with many young adults, and they have seen lives transformed as a result. The young adults they have touched are so thankful for being introduced to another world, a world much different from the one they were handed from the attempt to create a utopian society by the 1960s' radicals. Instead of ingratitude and victimhood, these young adults now embrace gratitude and personal responsibility. Instead of brokenness, they now experience healing and wholeness.

These are the actions that will point them back to God, provide them with direction, and slowly transform not only their lives, but our society as well. By investing in the generations to come, we can reclaim our culture and nation from the cultural and political morass of the 1960s. We will no longer be a nation alienated from each other, but one united with each other.

Our country can once again become the United States, instead of the divided states of America, despite whatever differences we may have. We can return to a nation of hope and opportunity instead of finger-pointing and despair. Only then can children regain the innocence of childhood, faith truly flourishing, and racial and cultural divides healed. That is the type of society I want, one that affirms human dignity and what the best of our fellow citizens, and I believe we all want for America and the world. While Utopia is an illusion ("not a place" in Greek), the American society formed under the First Principles established by our Declaration of Independence and original Constitution was proven true and can be again.

NOTES

INTRODUCTION

1. Robert O. Self, *All in the Family: The Realignment of American Democracy Since the 1960s* (New York: Hill and Wang, 2012), 3.
2. Melissa Erickson, "From Hope to Fear: The 1960s started comfortably—then we realized no one was safe," Columbus Dispatch, May 25, 2017, https://www.dispatch.com/story/lifestyle/2017/05/25/from-hope-to-fear-1960s/20784584007/ (Accessed August 1, 2023).
3. J. Harvie Wilkinson III, *All Falling Faiths: Reflections on the Promise and Failure of the 1960s* (New York: Encounter Books, 2017), x.
4. "Utopia," *Merriam-Webster.com Dictionary*, https://www.merriam-webster.com/dictionary/Utopia.
5. "Imagine," by John Lennon, *Imagine*, Apple, 1971, https://www.johnlennon.com/music/albums/imagine/.
6. Ashley R. Williams, "A Record-High Number of 40-Year-Olds in the US Have Never Been Married, Study Finds," CNN.com, July 1, 2023, https://www.cnn.com/2023/07/01/us/record-number-of-40-year-olds-never-married-trnd/index.html (Accessed August 29, 2023).
7. Kevin Boyle, *The Shattering: America in the 1960s* (New York: W.W. Norton and Company, 2021).
8. Self, *All in the Family*, 3.
9. Erickson, "From Hope to Fear."
10. James Jeffrey, "1968 Democratic Convention: 'A week of hate,'" BBC.com, August 27, 2018, https://www.bbc.com/news/world-us-canada-45226132 (Accessed August 1, 2023).

11. Kenneth T. Walsh, "1968: The Year That Changed America Forever," *U.S. News and World Report*, December 31, 2017, https://www.usnews.com/news/national-news/articles/2017-12-31/1968-the-year-that-changed-america-forever (Accessed August 1, 2023).
12. Steven M. Gillon, "The Revolution That Was 1968," History.com, February 23, 2018, https://www.history.com/news/the-revolution-that-was-1968 (Accessed August 1, 2023).
13. Wilkinson, *All Falling Faiths*, 171.
14. Aaron Zitner, "Americans Pull Back from Values That Once Defined U.S., WSJ-NORC Poll Finds," *Wall Street Journal*, March 27, 2023.
15. Zitner, "Americans Pull Back from Values."
16. John Uri, "50 Years Ago: One Small Step, One Giant Leap," NASA.gov., July 19, 2019, https://www.nasa.gov/feature/50-years-ago-one-small-step-one-giant-leap (Accessed August 1, 2023).

CHAPTER ONE

1. Myron Magnet, *The Dream and the Nightmare* (New York: Encounter Books, 2000), 34.
2. Kenneth Walsh, "The 1960s: Polarization, Cynicism, and the Youth Rebellion," *U.S. News and World Report*, March 12, 2010, https://www.usnews.com/news/articles/2010/03/12/the-1960s-polarization-cynicism-and-the-youth-rebellionredirect (Accessed August 1, 2023).

CHAPTER TWO

1. Hugh Gordon, "The Permanent Blight of Left-Wing Factions," *Washington Times*, February 17, 2023.
2. Herbert Marcuse, *Eros and Civilization* (Boston: Beacon Press, 1955).

3. Friedrich Nietzsche, *The Gay Science* (Chemnitz, Germany: Ernst Schmeitzner, 1882).

4. Gustavo Figueroa, "Nietzsche's Mental Disorders: Madness, Being Sick, 'How to Become What You Are,'" *Journal of Neuropsychiatry*, August 6, 2020, https://www.journalofneuropsychiatry.cl/docs/7/43.pdf.

5. Peggy Lamson, *Roger Baldwin, Founder of the American Civil Liberties Union: A Portrait* (Boston: Houghton-Mifflin, 1976), 63–64.

6. Lamson, *Roger Baldwin*, 192.

7. "The Senate Passes the Federal Reserve Act," United States Senate, https://www.senate.gov/artandhistory/history/minute/Senate_Passes_the_Federal_Reserve_Act.htm (Accessed August 1, 2023).

8. Ronald Pestritto, "Woodrow Wilson: Godfather of Liberalism," The Heritage Foundation, July 31, 2012, https://www.heritage.org/political-process/report/woodrow-wilson-godfather-liberalism (Accessed April 14, 2023).

9. "The Law: Emanations from a Penumbra," *Time*, June 18, 1965, https://content.time.com/time/magazine/article/0,9171,898883,00.html (Accessed April 16, 2023).

10. J. Roberts, dissent, *Obergefell v. Hodges*, Nos. 14–556, 14–562, 14–571, and 14–574, June 26, 2015.

11. Ronald J. Pestritto, "Why the Early Progressives Rejected American Founding Principles," RealClearPublicAffairs, https://www.realclearpublicaffairs.com/articles/2021/06/08/why_the_early_progressives_rejected_american_founding_principles_779946.html (Accessed May 1, 2023).

12. Pestritto, "Why the Early Progressives Rejected American Founding Principles."

13. Pestritto, "Woodrow Wilson: Godfather of Liberalism."

14. James Bovard, "Woodrow Wilson the World Unsafe for Democracy," Foundation for Economic Education, April 6,

2017, https://fee.org/articles/woodrow-wilson-made-the-world-unsafe-for-democracy/ (Accessed May 5, 2023).

15. R. Albert Mohler Jr., "The New Left and the Radical Transformation of America," World, June 15, 2022.

16. Students for a Democratic Society, "The Port Huron Statement," 58–59. http://www.progressivefox.com/misc_documents/PortHuronStatement.pdf

17. Ibid., 63.

18. Ibid., 62.

19. Ibid., 29.

20. Ibid., 32.

21. Mohler, "The New Left and the Radical Transformation of America."

22. Mohler, "The New Left and the Radical Transformation of America."

23. Howard Brick and Gregory Parker, eds., *A New Insurgency: The Port Huron Statement and Its Times* (Ann Arbor: Maize Books, Michigan Publishing Services, 2015), 111.

24. Amity Shlaes, *Great Society: A New History* (New York: HarperCollins, 2019), 73.

25. Myron Magnet, *The Dream and the Nightmare* (New York: Encounter Books, 2000), 16.

26. Magnet, 16.

27. Magnet, 35.

28. Roger L. Simon, "Moral Narcissism and the Least-Great Generation," *Commentary*, June 2016, https://www.commentary.org/articles/roger-simon/moral-narcissism-least-great-generation/.

29. Simon, "Moral Narcissism and the Least-Great Generation."

30. Simon, "Moral Narcissism and the Least-Great Generation."

31. Cited in Paul Kengor, "Saul Alinsky: Playing Merry Hell," *Crisis Magazine*, October 13, 2020, https://crisismagazine.com/opinion/saul-alinsky-playing-merry-hell (Accessed February 27, 2023).

32. Wayne Laugesen, "The Godfather: How Saul Alinsky went from Al Capone underling to godfather of political chaos," *Washington Examiner*, January 4, 2019, https://www.washingtonexaminer.com/politics/the-godfather.

33. Laugesen, "The Godfather."

34. Saul Alinsky, *Rules for Radicals: A Practical Primer for Realistic Radicals* (New York: Vintage Books Edition, 1989), 131–34, https://chisineu.files.wordpress.com/2014/02/saul-alinsky-rules-for-radicals-1989.pdf (Accessed February 25, 2023).

35. Alinsky, *Rules for Radicals*, 134.

36. Cited in Noam Cohen, "Know Thine Enemy," *New York Times*, August 23, 2009, https://www.nytimes.com/2009/08/23/weekinreview/23alinsky.html (Accessed August 2, 2023).

37. Richard Andrew Cloward and Frances Fox Piven, "The Weight of the Poor: A Strategy to End Poverty," May 2, 1966 *The Nation*, https://www.thenation.com/article/archive/weight-poor-strategy-end-poverty/

CHAPTER THREE

1. Judith A. Reisman and Edward W. Eichel, *Kinsey, Sex and Fraud: The Indoctrination of a People* (Lafayette, LA: Lochinvar-Huntington House, 1990).

2. Mary Eberstadt, *Adam and Eve after the Pill, Revisited* (San Francisco: Ignatius Press, 2023), 63.

3. Sue Ellin Browder, "Kinsey's Secret: The Phony Science of the Sexual Revolution," *Crisis Magazine*, May 28, 2012, https://crisismagazine.com/opinion/kinseys-secret-the-phony-science-of-the-sexual-revolution (Accessed May 15, 2023).

4. Browder, "Kinsey's Secret."

5. Browder, "Kinsey's Secret."

6. Carl Trueman, *Strange New World: How Thinkers and Activists Redefined Identity and Sparked the Sexual Revolution* (Wheaton, IL: Crossway, 2022), 105.
7. Anne Hendershott, *The Politics of Deviance* (San Francisco: Encounter Books, 2002), 3.
8. Hendershott, The Politics of Deviance, 6.
9. Alan F. Guttmacher, "Clinical Analysis," *New York Times*, May 29, 1966, https://www.nytimes.com/books/97/03/23/reviews/bright-response.html?scp=1&sq=Epigastrium&st=cse (Accessed March 28, 2023).
10. Yuval Levin, *The Fractured Republic: Renewing America's Social Contract in the Age of Individualism* (New York: Basic Books, 2016), 68.
11. Trueman, *Strange New World*, 102.
12. "The Great Bluff That Led to a 'Magical' Pill And Sexual Revolution," National Public Radio, October 2, 2015, https://www.npr.org/sections/health-shots/2014/10/07/354103536/the-great-bluff-that-lead-to-a-magical-pill-and-a-sexual-revolution (Accessed March 29, 2023).
13. "The Great Bluff."
14. Glenn T. Stanton, "The Pill: Did It Cause the Sexual Revolution?" July 6, 2010, https://www.focusonthefamily.com/marriage/the-pill-did-it-cause-the-sexual-revolution/.
15. Ralf Bosen, "The Pill at 60—Transformative and Controversial," DW.com, August 16, 2020 https://www.dw.com/en/the-pill-birth-control-contraceptive-anniversary/a-54573038 (Accessed April 1, 2023).

CHAPTER FOUR

1. Wayne Laugesen, "The Godfather: How Saul Alinsky went from Al Capone underling to godfather of political chaos," *Washington Examiner*, January 4, 2019, https://www.washingtonexaminer.com/politics/the-godfather.

2. Terresa Monroe-Hamilton, "Florida Teacher Slams Parental Rights: 'Those Rights are Gone When Your Child Is in the Public School System," *BBR Business and Politics*, May 17, 2023, https://www.bizpacreview.com/2023/05/17/fla-teacher-slams-parental-rights-those-rights-are-gone-when-your-child-is-in-the-public-school-system-1359859/ (Accessed May 18, 2023).

3. Jarrett Stepman, "Americans Have Almost Entirely Forgotten Their History," *Daily Signal*, October 4, 2018, https://www.dailysignal.com/2018/10/04/american-have-almost-entirely-forgotten-their-history/ (Accessed May 20, 2020).

4. Stepman, "American Have Almost Entirely Forgotten Their History."

5. "Adult Literacy Facts," https://www.proliteracy.org/Adult-Literacy-Facts (Accessed August 1, 2023).

6. Amy Rea, "How Serious Is America's Literacy Problem," *Library Journal*, April 29, 2020, https://www.library journal.com/story/How-Serious-Is-Americas-Literacy-Problem (Accessed July 1, 2023).

7. Cited in "Illiteracy in America: Troubling Statistics and How Schools Can Help," Resilient Educator, March 9, 2018, https://resilienteducator.com/news/illiteracy-in-america/ (Accessed July 1, 2023).

8. John Dewey, "The Relation of Theory to Practice in Education" in C. A. McMurry, ed., *The Relation Between Theory and Practice in the Education of Teachers: Third Yearbook of the National Society for the Scientific Study of Education* (Chicago: University of Chicago Press, 1904).

9. Henry T. Edmonson III, *John Dewey and the Decline of American Education* (Wilmington, DE: ISI Books, 2006), 2.

10. John Dewey, Text of speech to Teachers College at Columbia University can be accessed here: http://www.yorku.ca/rsheese2/3410/utopia.htm.

11. Edmonson III, *John Dewey and the Decline of American Education*, 7.

12. John Dewey, *Human Nature and Conduct: An Introduction to Social Psychology* (New York: Henry Holt and Company, 1922), 330–31.

13. Edmonson III, *John Dewey and the Decline of American Education*, 19.

14. Dewey, *Human Nature and Conduct*, 297; John Dewey, *Experience and Education* (Kappa Delta Pi, 1938), 221.

15. Dewey, Human Nature and Conduct, 296.

16. Edmonson III, *John Dewey and the Decline of American Education*, 20.

17. John Dewey, *Liberalism and Social Action* (New York: G.P. Putnam, 1935).

18. John Dewey, *Democracy and Education* (UK: MacMillan Company, 1916), 387.

19. Edmondson, *John Dewey and the Decline of American Education*, 21.

20. *Engel v. Vitale*, 370 U.S. 421 (1962), https://supreme.justia.com/cases/federal/us/370/421/ (Accessed August 3, 2023).

21. *School District of Abington Township v. Schempp.* 374 U.S. 203 (1963) https://supreme.justia.com/cases/federal/us/374/203/ (Accessed August 3, 2023).

22. John Dewey, *Impressions of Soviet Russia and the Revolutionary World* (New York: New Republic, 1929), 57.

23. John Dewey, "The Primary-Education Fetish," Forum (1898), 315–28.

24. Ulrich Boser, Perpetual Baffour, and Steph Vela, "A Look at the Education Crisis: Tests, Students, and the Future of American Education, Center for American Progress, January 2016, https://cdn.americanprogress.org/wp-content/uploads/2016/01/21075127/TUDAreport.pdf (Accessed August 3, 2023).

25. Karen Harris, "New Math: The Curriculum That Failed Students and Teachers," GroovyHistory.com, https://groovyhistory.com/remember-new-math (Accessed June 1, 2023).

26. James McGeever, "The Decline of Standardized Test Scores in the United States from 1965 to the Present," October 1993, https://files.eric.ed.gov/fulltext/ED252565.pdf (Accessed May 15, 2023).

CHAPTER FIVE

1. Kathryn Montgomery, *Target: Prime Time* (Oxford: Oxford University Press, 1989), 5.

2. Myron Magnet, *The Dream and the Nightmare* (New York: Encounter Books, 2000), 15.

3. Jonathan Merritt, "10 Shows That Forced Us to Reimagine the American Family," September 11, 2013, https://www.jonathanmerritt.com/article/10-tv-shows-that-forced-us-to-reimagine-family (Accessed May 1, 2023).

4. Jim Harris, "You May Remember Him As Mr. Haney, But There's a Lot More to Pat Buttram," The Southern Voice.com, October 3, 2022, https://thesouthernvoice.com/you-may-remember-him-as-mr-haney-but-theres-a-lot-more-to-pat-buttram/ (Accessed May 14, 2023).

5. Stephen M. Gillon, "The Revolution That Was 1968," History.com, January 31, 2019, https://www.history.com/news/the-revolution-that-was-1968 (Accessed May 15, 2023).

6. R. Albert Mohler Jr., "Television's Boundary-Smashing Pioneer Turns 100," *World*, July 29, 2022, https://wng.org/opinions/televisions-boundary-smashing-pioneer-turns-100-1659090347 (Accessed July 30, 2022).

7. Montgomery, *Target: Prime Time*, 6.

8. Brian Alan Burhoe, "Rural Purge: The Day Hollywood Killed the Great Conservative Comedies & Westerns,"

CivilizedBears.com, February 10, 2019, https://www
.civilizedbears.com/rural-purge-day-hollywood-killed-
great-conservative-comedies-westerns/ (Accessed March 28,
2023).

9. Mohler, "Television's Boundary-Smashing Pioneer
Turns 100."

10. Marc Berman, "All in the Family Turns 50," *Forbes*,
January 12, 2021, https://www.forbes.com/sites/
marcberman1/2021/01/12/all-in-the-family-turns-50/
(Accessed March 1, 2023).

11. Norman Lear. "Exclusive Norman Lear Memoir Excerpt:
Throwdowns with Carroll O'Connor, Race Battles on
'Good Times,'" *The Hollywood Reporter*, October 2,
2014, http://www.hollywoodreporter.com/news/
norman-lear-memoir-excerpt-throwdowns-736647
(Accessed February 27, 2023).

12. Lou Haviland, "All in the Family's Creator Said the Show
Was His 'Love Letter' to His Father," July 16, 2021,
https://www.cheatsheet.com/entertainment/all-in-the-
familys-creator-show-love-letter-father.html/ (Accessed
August 3, 2023).

13. "Maude's Dilemma," Aired November 14 and 21, 1972,
https://www.imdb.com/title/tt0644325/ (Accessed
June 1, 2023).

14. Norman Lear, *Even This I Get to Experience* (New York:
Penguin Books, 2015), 235.

15. "Remarks by the President at Presentation of the National
Medal of the Arts and the National Humanities Medal,"
September 29, 1999, https://clintonwhitehouse4.archives.
gov/textonly/WH/New/html/19990929.html (Accessed
July 10, 2023).

16. "Norman Lear," DiscovertheNetworks.com, https://www
.discoverthenetworks.org/individuals/norman-lear/
(Accessed May 1, 2023).

17. "I Love Liberty," Aired March 21, 1982 https://www
.imdb.com/title/tt0304178/ (Accessed March 15, 2023).

18. Rafael Abreu, "What Is the Hays Code—Hollywood Production Code Explained," StudioBinder.com, May 2, 2021, https://www.studiobinder.com/blog/what-is-the-hays-code-1934/ (Accessed February 1, 2023).
19. Kristen Hunt, "Hollywood Codebreakers: 'Spartacus' Breaks the Blacklist," *Medium*, October 13, 2018, https://medium.com/@kristinhunt/spartacus-breaks-the-blacklist-f80e3c61d5cb (Accessed August 3, 2023).
20. Joseph Gelmis, "An Interview with Stanley Kubrick," 1969, http://www.visual-memory.co.uk/amk/doc/0069.html (Accessed July 1, 2023).
21. Chris Heckmann, "What Is New Hollywood? The Revolution of 1960s and '70s Hollywood," StudioBinder.com, May 17, 2020, https://www.studiobinder.com/blog/what-is-new-hollywood/ (Accessed March 15, 2023).
22. Mark Powell, "Kinsey and Hef," TheSpectator.au.com, October 10, 2017, https://www.spectator.com.au/2017/10/kinsey-and-hef/ (Accessed July 26, 2023).
23. Kira Wang, "Playboy Bunnies, Hugh Hefner, and the Commodification of Sexual Abuse," 34st.com, February 28, 2022, http://www.34st.com/article/2022/02/playboy-bunny-playmate-mansion-hugh-hefner-sexual-exploitation-abuse-violence-sex-logo.
24. Mary Eberstadt, *Adam and Eve after the Pill*, Revisited (San Francisco: Ignatius Press, 2023), 44.
25. Kate N. Grossman, "'Hugh Hefner Way' Wins Approval of Chicago Board," Associated Press, April 12, 2000, https://www.southcoasttoday.com/story/entertainment/local/2000/04/12/hugh-hefner-way-wins/50491572007/ (Accessed May 1, 2023).
26. Marco Margaritoff, "The Complete, Unadulterated History of 1969's Woodstock Music Festival," Allthatsinteresting.com, July 11, 2019, https://allthatsinteresting.com/woodstock-festival-1969 (Accessed June 1, 2023).
27. Tony Sclafani, "Debunking Woodstock: What really happened?," Today.com, August 10, 2009, https://www

.today.com/popculture/debunking-woodstock-what-really-happened-2d80555859 (Accessed April 16, 2023).

28. Margaritoff, "The Complete, Unadulterated History of Woodstock."

29. Barbara Maranzani, "10 Things You May Not Know About Woodstock," April 23, 2013 https://www.history.com/news/remembering-richie-havens-ten-things-you-may-not-know-about-woodstock

30. Sclafani, "Debunking Woodstock."

31. Owen Gleiberman, "Altamont at 45: The most dangerous rock concert," BBC Culture.com, February 24, 2022, https://www.bbc.com/culture/article/20141205-did-altamont-end-the-60s (Accessed May 2, 2023).

32. Gleiberman, "Altamont at 45."

CHAPTER SIX

1. Robert Higgs, "The Economics of the Great Society," February 1, 2011, Independent Institute, February 1, 2011, https://www.independent.org/publications/article.asp?id=3157 (Accessed April 14, 2023).

2. Kimberly Amadeo, "U.S. National Debt by Year," TheBalanceMoney.com, January 18, 2023, https://www.thebalancemoney.com/national-debt-by-year-compared-to-gdp-and-major-events-3306287 (Accessed April 28, 2023).

3. "United States Inflation Rate in 1979," https://www.statbureau.org/en/united-states/inflation/1979 (Accessed August 1, 2023).

4. Mike Moffatt, "Fiscal Policy in the 1960s and 1970s," TheThoughtCo.com, January 27, 2020, https://www.thoughtco.com/fiscal-policy-in-the-1960s-and-1970s-1147748 (Accessed March 29, 2023).

5. Rachel Sheffield and Robert Rector, "The War on Poverty after 50 Years," The Heritage Foundation, September 15,

2014, https://www.heritage.org/poverty-and-inequality/report/the-war-poverty-after-50-years.

6. "Lyndon Johnson's Great Society Speech," May 22, 1964, https://www.ushistory.org/documents/great_society.htm (Accessed June 1, 2023).

7. Sheffield and Rector, "The War on Poverty after 50 Years."

8. "Government Spending in Historical Context," https://www.ntu.org/foundation/tax-page/government-spending-in-historical-context (accessed April 5, 2023).

9. Sheffield and Rector, "The War on Poverty after 50 Years."

10. Sheffield and Rector, "The War on Poverty after 50 Years."

11. James Pethokoukis, "Tallying the Costs and Benefits of LBJ's Great Society," American Enterprise Institute, April 4, 2016, https://www.aei.org/economics/public-economics/tallying-the-costs-and-benefits-of-lbjs-great-society/ (Accessed April 16, 2023).

12. Sally Pipes, "Medicare and Medicaid Turn 56 Today. That's Not a Cause for Celebration," *Forbes*, July 30, 2021, https://www.forbes.com/sites/sallypipes/2021/07/30/medicare-and-medicaid-turn-56-today-thats-not-exactly-cause-for-celebration/ (Accessed June 4, 2023).

13. Pipes, "Medicare and Medicaid Turn 56 Today."

14. "Medicare Financial Status In Brief," Congressional Research Service, October 21, 2021 https://crsreports.congress.gov/product/pdf/R/R43122

15. Laura Hollis, "The Failed Legacy of Johnson's 'Great Society,'" Creators Syndicate, June 23, 2022, https://www.creators.com/read/laura-hollis/06/22/the-failed-legacy-of-johnsons-great-society (Accessed February 1, 2023).

16. Pethokoukis, "Tallying the Costs."

17. Robert Higgs, "The Economics of the Great Society."

18. Paul K. Conkin, *Big Daddy from the Pedernales: Lyndon Baines Johnson* (Boston: Twayne Publishers, 1986), 209.

19. Conkin, *Big Daddy from the Pedernales.*

20. Henry J. Aaron, *Politics and the Professors: The Great Society in Perspective* (Washington, D.C.: Brookings Institution, 1978), 3.
21. Sheffield and Rector, "The War on Poverty after 50 Years."
22. *Animal Crackers* (1930), Paramount Pictures.
23. Sheffield and Rector, "The War on Poverty after 50 Years."
24. Sheffield and Rector, "The War on Poverty after 50 Years."
25. Sheffield and Rector, "The War on Poverty after 50 Years."
26. Amity Shlaes, *Great Society: A New History* (New York: Harper-Collins, 2019), 10.
27. Shlaes, *Great Society*, 11.
28. Shlaes, 4.
29. Alan Greenspan and Adrian Wooldridge, Capitalism in America: A History (New York: Penguin, 2018), 365.
30. Shlaes, Great Society, 7.
31. Shlaes, 10.
32. Shlaes, 14.
33. Lindsey Burke, "Equipping American Workers and Families to Thrive," RealClearHealth.com, September 25, 2020, https://www.realclearhealth.com/articles/2020/09/25/equipping_american_workers_and_families_to_thrive__111110.html (Accessed March 16, 2023).

CHAPTER SEVEN

1. Thomas Sowell, "A Legacy of Liberalism," Creators Syndicate, November 18, 2014, https://www.creators.com/read/thomas-sowell/11/14/a-legacy-of-liberalism (Accessed March 31, 2023).
2. W. Bradford Wilcox, "The Evolution of Divorce," *National Affairs*, Fall 2019, https://www.nationalaffairs.com/publications/detail/the-evolution-of-divorce (Accessed March 15, 2023).
3. "The American family today," Pew Research Center, December 17, 2015, https://www.pewresearch.org/

social-trends/2015/12/17/1-the-american-family-today/ (Accessed January 28, 2023).

4. Alicia VanOrman and Linda A. Jacobsen, "U.S. Household Composition Shifts as the Population Grows Older; More Young Adults Live with Parents," Population Research Bureau, February 12, 2020, https://www.prb.org/ resources/u-s-household-composition-shifts-as-the-population-grows-older-more-young-adults-live-with-parents/.

5. Ron Haskins, "The War on Poverty: What Went Wrong?" Brookings Institute, November 19, 2013, https://www .brookings.edu/articles/the-war-on-poverty-what-went-wrong/ (Accessed February 27, 2023).

6. Haskins, "The War on Poverty."

7. Daniel Moynihan, Speech at University of Chicago, 1992.

8. "Births: Final Data for 2021," *National Vital Statistics Reports* 72, no. 1 (January 31, 2023) https://www.cdc .gov/nchs/data/nvsr/nvsr72/nvsr72-01-tables.pdf (Accessed March 8, 2023).

9. Jason L. Riley, "Still Right on the Black Family After All These Years," *Wall Street Journal*, February 10, 2015, http://online.wsj.com/articles/jason-l-riley-still-right-on-the-black-family-after-all-these-years-1423613625 (Accessed March 14, 2023).

10. Riley, "Still Right."

11. David R. Francis, "How the 1960s' Riots Hurt African Americans," *National Bureau of Economic Research*, September 2004, https://www.nber.org/digest/sep04/ how-1960s-riots-hurt-african-americans (Accessed March 19, 2023).

12. Myron Magnet, *The Dream and the Nightmare* (New York: Encounter Books, 2000), 30.

13. Paul Peterson, "A Rescue Plan for the Black Family," *New York Daily News*, January 19, 2015, https://www

.nydailynews.com/opinion/paul-peterson-rescue-plan-black-family-article-1.2081833.

14. Peterson, "A Rescue Plan."

15. Steven Pinker, "Decivilization in the 1960s," *Human Figurations* 2, no. 2, July 2013, https://quod.lib.umich.edu/h/humfig/11217607.0002.206/--decivilization-in-the-1960s?rgn=main;view=fulltext (Accessed February 16, 2023).

16. Willis Krumholz, "Family Breakdown and America's Welfare System," *Institute for Family Studies*, October 7, 2019, https://ifstudies.org/blog/family-breakdown-and-americas-welfare-system (Accessed March 5, 2023).

17. Krumholz, "Family Breakdown."

18. Krumholz, "Family Breakdown."

19. Paul Ehrlich, *The Population Bomb* (Cutchogue, NY: Buccaneer Books, 1968).

20. James Gallagher, "Fertility rate: 'Jaw-dropping' global crash in children being born," BBC.com, July 15, 2020, https://www.bbc.com/news/health-53409521 (Accessed February 16, 2023).

21. Gallagher, "Fertility rate."

22. Derek Thompson, "Why U.S. Population Growth Is Collapsing," *The Atlantic*, March 28, 2022, https://www.theatlantic.com/newsletters/archive/2022/03/american-population-growth-rate-slow/629392/ (accessed May 10, 2023).

23. Tyler J. VanderWeele, "Religious Service Attendance, Marriage, and Health," Institute for Family Studies, November 29, 2016, https://ifstudies.org/blog/religious-service-attendance-marriage-and-health (Accessed June 1, 2023).

24. W. Bradford Wilcox, "The Marriage Divide: How and Why Working-class Families Are More Fragile Today," American Enterprise Institute, September 25, 2017, https://ifstudies.

org/blog/the-marriage-divide-how-and-why-working-class-families-are-more-fragile-today (Accessed December 10, 2022).

25. Paul Hemez and Chanell Washington, "Number of Kids Living Only with Their Mothers Has Doubled in 50 Years," Census.gov, April 12, 2021, https://www.census.gov/library/stories/2021/04/number-of-children-living-only-with-their-mothers-has-doubled-in-past-50-years.html.

26. Robert Rector, "Marriage: America's Greatest Weapon Against Child Poverty," The Heritage Foundation, September 16, 2010, https://www.heritage.org/poverty-and-inequality/report/marriage-americas-greatest-weapon-against-child-poverty-0 (Accessed March 1, 2023).

27. Magnet, *The Dream and the Nightmare*, 53.

28. Magnet, 54.

29. Wilcox, "The Evolution of Divorce."

30. Wilcox, "The Evolution of Divorce."

31. Wilcox, "The Evolution of Divorce."

32. Wilcox, "The Evolution of Divorce."

33. Wilcox, "The Evolution of Divorce."

34. W. H. Jeynes, "The effects of recent parental divorce on their children's sexual attitudes and behavior," *Journal of Divorce and Remarriage* 35 (2001): 125.

35. B. J. Ellis et al., "Does father absence place daughters at special risk for early sexual activity and teenage pregnancy?" *Child Dev* 74 (2003): 810–11.

36. D. J. Weigel, "Parental divorce and the types of commitment-related messages people gain from their families of origin," *Journal of Divorce and Remarriage* 47 (2007): 23.

37. "America's Families and Living Arrangements: 2021," Census.gov, November 29, 2021, https://www.census.gov/newsroom/press-releases/2021/families-and-living-arrangements.html (Accessed April 1, 2023).

38. "Census Bureau Releases New Estimates on America's Families and Living Arrangements," Census.gov, November

29, 2021, https://www.census.gov/newsroom/press-releases/2021/families-and-living-arrangements.html (Accessed April 1, 2023).

39. "Census Bureau Releases New Estimates."

40. Esther Lee, "This Is the Average Age of Marriage in America," April 17, 2023, https://www.theknot.com/content/average-age-of-marriage (Accessed September 13, 2023).

41. Ashley R. Williams, "A Record Number of 40-Year-Olds Have Never Been Married," CNN.com, July 1, 2023, https://www.cnn.com/2023/07/01/us/record-number-of-40-year-olds-never-married-trnd/index.html (Accessed September 13, 2013).

42. Williams, "Record Number."

43. Williams, "Record Number."

44. Williams, "Record Number."

45. John Cacioppo, *Loneliness: Human Nature and the Need for Social Connection* (New York: W.W. Norton & Co, 2009).

46. Douglas Belkin, "A Generation of Men Give Up on College: 'I Just Feel Lost," *Wall Street Journal*, September 6, 2021, https://www.wsj.com/articles/college-university-fall-higher-education-men-women-enrollment-admissions-back-to-school-11630948233 (Accessed September 15, 2023).

47. Belkin, "A Generation of Men Give Up on College."

48. Rector, "Marriage: America's Greatest Weapon Against Child Poverty."

49. Catherine St. Louis, "Rise in Infant Drug Dependence in U.S. Is Felt Mostly in Rural Areas," *New York Times*, December 12, 2016, https://www.nytimes.com/2016/12/12/health/rise-in-infant-drug-dependence-in-us-is-felt-most-in-rural-areas.html (Accessed November 1, 2018).

50. St. Louis, "Rise in Infant Drug Dependence."
51. Deborah Savage, "The Return of the Madman: Nietzsche, Nihilism, and the Death of God, circa 2020," *Catholic World Report*, August 10, 2020, https://www.catholicworldreport.com/2020/08/10/the-return-of-the-madman-nietzsche-nihilism-and-the-death-of-god-circa-2020/ (Accessed June 5, 2023).
52. Mary Meehan, "ACLU vs. Unborn Children," *Human Life Review*, Spring 2001.
53. Meehan, citing Barbara J. Syska and others, "An Objective Model for Eliminating Criminal Abortions and Its Implications for Public Policy," *New Perspectives on Human Abortion* (Frederick, MD: University Publications of America, 1981), 164–81.
54. Meehan, citing Cynthia McKnight, *Life Without Roe: Making Predictions About Illegal Abortions* (Washington D.C.: Horatio R. Storer Foundation, 1992).

CHAPTER EIGHT

1. J. Harvie Wilkinson III, *All Falling Faiths: Reflections on the Promise and Failure of the 1960s* (New York: Encounter Books, 2017), 163.
2. Kevin DeYoung, "Lessons from Mainline Decline," World.org, May 2, 2022, https://wng.org/opinions/lessons-from-mainline-decline-1651490979 (Accessed February 1, 2023).
3. Mary Eberstadt, *Adam and Eve after the Pill, Revisited* (San Francisco: Ignatius Press, 2023), 53.
4. DeYoung, "Lessons from Mainline Decline."
5. Yuval Levin, *The Fractured Republic: Renewing America's Social Contract in the Age of Individualism* (New York: Basic Books, 2016), 65.
6. Philip Jenkins, "The Religious World Changed in 1968, but Not in the Ways We Think," ABC Religion & Ethics, July

30, 2018, https://www.abc.net.au/religion/the-religious-world-changed-in-1968-but-not-in-the-ways-we-think/10214328.

7. Levin, *The Fractured Republic*, 66.

8. Wilkinson, *All Falling Faiths*, 169.

9. Aaron Earls, "Protestant Church Closures Outpace Openings in U.S.," Lifeway Research, May 25, 2021, https://research.lifeway.com/2021/05/25/protestant-church-closures-outpace-openings-in-u-s/ (Accessed March 16, 2023).

10. Richard Reinhard, "Redeveloping Houses of Worship," ICMA.com, April 1, 2021, https://icma.org/articles/pm-magazine/redeveloping-houses-worship (Accessed January 31, 2023).

11. Jeffrey Jones, "U.S. Church Membership Falls Below Majority for First Time," Gallup.com, March 29, 2021, https://news.gallup.com/poll/341963/church-membership-falls-below-majority-first-time.aspx (Accessed June 14, 2023.

12. Jones, "U.S. Church Membership Falls."

13. Ryan P. Burge, "Nondenominational Churches Are Adding Millions of Members," *Christianity Today*, August 5, 2022, https://www.christianitytoday.com/news/2022/august/nondenominational-growth-mainline-protestant-decline-survey.html (Accessed March 29, 2023).

14. Mark Tooley, "Don't celebrate the decline of mainline churches," *Christian Post*, April 29, 2022, https://www.christianpost.com/voices/dont-celebrate-the-decline-of-mainline-churches.html (Accessed April 14, 2023).

15. Joe Carter, "FactChecker: Are All Christian Denominations in Decline?" The Gospel Coalition, March 17, 2015, https://www.thegospelcoalition.org/article/factchecker-are-all-christian-denominations-in-decline/ (Accessed February 1, 2023).

16. Carter, "FactChecker."

17. Ross Douthat, *Bad Religion: How We Became a Nation of Heretics* (New York: Free Press, 2012), 62.
18. Levin, *The Fractured Republic*, 160.
19. Levin, 162.
20. Joanne Beckman, "Religion in Post-World War II America, The Twentieth Century, Divining America: Religion in American History," https://nationalhumanitiescenter.org/tserve/twenty/tkeyinfo/trelww2.htm (Accessed April 3, 2023).
21. "Modeling the Future of Religion in America," Pew Research Center, September 13, 2022, https://www.pewresearch.org/religion/2022/09/13/modeling-the-future-of-religion-in-america/ (Accessed March 16, 2023).
22. Daniel A. Cox, "Generation Z and the Future of Faith in America," March 24, 2022, https://www.americansurveycenter.org/research/generation-z-future-of-faith/ (Accessed April 17, 2023).
23. Juliana Menasce Horowitz, Nikki Graf, and Gretchen Livingston, "The state of marriage and cohabitation in the U.S.," Pew Research Center, November 6, 2019, https://www.pewresearch.org/social-trends/2019/11/06/the-landscape-of-marriage-and-cohabitation-in-the-u-s/ (Accessed March 4, 2023).
24. David Ayers, "Cohabitation Among Evangelicals: A New Norm?" Institute for Family Studies, April 19, 2021, https://ifstudies.org/blog/cohabitation-among-evangelicals-a-new-norm (Accessed February 1, 2023).
25. Ayers, "Cohabitation Among Evangelicals."
26. David Keene, "In today's America, the future for conservatives looks bright," *Washington Times*, June 12, 2023, https://www.washingtontimes.com/news/2023/jun/12/in-todays-america-future-for-conservatives-looks-b/.

CHAPTER NINE

1. J. Harvie Wilkinson III, *All Falling Faiths: Reflections on the Promise and Failure of the 1960s* (New York: Encounter Books, 2017), 176.
2. Brink Lindsey, "The Loss of Faith," February 21, 2023, https://brinklindsey.substack.com/p/the-loss-of-faith (Accessed June 1, 2023).
3. Megan Brenan, "Record-Low 38% Extremely Proud to Be American," Gallup.org, June 29, 2022, https://news.gallup.com/poll/394202/record-low-extremely-proud-american.aspx (Accessed April 1, 2023).
4. Matt Seyler, "Military struggling to find new troops as fewer young Americans willing or able to serve," ABCNews.com, July 2, 2022, https://abcnews.go.com/Politics/military-struggling-find-troops-fewer-young-americans-serve/story?id=86067103 (Accessed March 19, 2023).
5. "Inaugural Address of Ronald Reagan, Governor of California, January 5, 1967," https://www.reaganlibrary.gov/archives/speech/january-5-1967-inaugural-address-public-ceremony (Accessed January 15, 2023).
6. Brenan, "Record-Low 38% Extremely Proud to Be American."
7. Ingrid Jacques, "Gen Z Doesn't Love the US Like Boomers Do. That Doesn't Bode Well for the Future," *USA Today*, August 1, 2023, https://www.usatoday.com/story/opinion/columnists/2023/08/01/gen-z-patriotic-negative-views-capitalism/70473580007/ (Accessed August 1, 2023).
8. Nadra Kareem Nittle, "Why Black American Athletes Raised Their Fists at the 1968 Olympics," History.com, May 25, 2021, https://www.history.com/news/black-athletes-raise-fists-1968-olympics (Accessed August 4, 2023).
9. Thomas Carothers and Andrew O'Donohue, "How Americans Were Driven to Extremes," *Foreign Affairs*,

September 25, 2019, https://www.foreignaffairs.com/
articles/united-states/2019-09-25/how-americans-were-
driven-extremes (Accessed July 7, 2021).

10. Jennifer Harper, "47% of Americans 'Feel Like a Stranger in
    Their Own Country,'" *Washington Times*, November 1,
    2018, https://www.washingtontimes.com/news/2018/
    nov/1/47-of-americans-feel-like-a-stranger-in-their-own/
    (Accessed November 11, 2020).

11. "31 Percent Think U.S. Civil War Likely Soon," Rasmussen
    Reports, June 27, 2018, https://www.rasmussenreports.
    com/public_content/politics/general_politics/
    june_2018/31_think_u_s_civil_war_likely_soon (Accessed
    March 4, 2023).

12. Dante Chinni and Sally Bronston, "Americans are divided
    over everything except division," NBCNews.com, October
    21, 2018, https://www.nbcnews.com/politics/first-read/
    americans-are-divided-over-everything-except-division
    -n922511 (Accessed July 31, 2023).

13. Glenn Harlan Reynolds, "Is America Headed Toward a Civil
    War?" USA Today, June 25, 2018, https://www.usatoday
    .com/story/opinion/2018/06/25/sanders-nielsen-
    incidents-suggest-new-us-civil-war-underway-column/
    729141002/.

14. Wilkinson, *All Falling Faiths*, 175.

15. David Greenberg, "Here's What Happened the Last Time
    the Left Got Nasty," Politico, July 5, 2018, https://www.
    politico.com/magazine/story/2018/07/05/democrats-
    civility-1960s-violence-218948 (Accessed December 29,
    2022).

16. Greenberg, "Here's What Happened."

17. Greenberg, "Here's What Happened."

CHAPTER TEN

1. Myron Magnet, *The Dream and the Nightmare* (New York: Encounter Books, 2000), 34.
2. Shawn Parr, "How Ideas From the 1960s Prevail in Leadership, Art, Design, and Socia," *Fast Company*, March 8, 2012, https://www.fastcompany.com/1823202/how-ideas-1960s-prevail-leadership-art-design-and-social-movements (Accessed December 20, 2023).
3. J. Harvie Wilkinson III, *All Falling Faiths: Reflections on the Promise and Failure of the 1960s* (New York: Encounter Books, 2017), xi.
4. "The Sixties," AP US History Study Guide from The Gilder Lehrman Institute of American History https://ap.gilderlehrman.org/history-by-era/sixties/essays/sixties (Accessed January 22, 2023).
5. Wilkinson, *All Falling Faiths*, xii.
6. Jeffrey M. Jones, "Social Conservatism in U.S Highest in Almost a Decade," Gallup.com, June 8, 2023, https://news.gallup.com/poll/506765/social-conservatism-highest-decade.aspx (Accessed June 9, 2023).
7. Jones, "Social Conservatism."
8. David Keene, "In today's America, the future for conservatives looks bright," *Washington Times*, June 12, 2023, https://www.washingtontimes.com/news/2023/jun/12/in-todays-america-future-for-conservatives-looks-b/.
9. Carl R. Trueman, *The Rise and Triumph of the Modern Self* (Wheaton, IL: Crossway, 2020), 30.

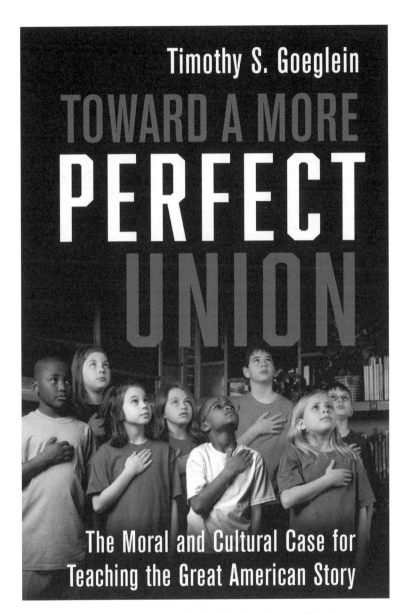

Timothy S. Goeglein

TOWARD A MORE
PERFECT
UNION

The Moral and Cultural Case for
Teaching the Great American Story

*Toward a More Perfect Union: The Moral and Cultural Case for
Teaching the Great American Story*
—9781956454130 Hardcover/9781956454147 eBook

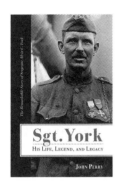

Sgt. York His Life, Legend, and Legacy: The Remarkable Story of Sergeant Alvin C. York—
9781735856322-Paperback
9781735856339 eBook

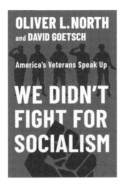

We Didn't Fight for Socialism: America's Veterans Speak Up—
9781735856346 Hardcover/
9781735856353 eBook

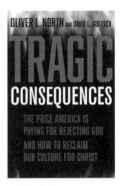

Tragic Consequences: The Price America is Paying for Rejecting God and How to Reclaim Our Culture for Christ—
9781956454000 Hardcover/
9781956454017 eBook

America's Endgame For the 21st Century: A Blueprint for Saving Our Country—
9781956454178 Hardcover/
9781956454185 eBook

Drawing Lines: Why Conservatives Must Begin to Battle Fiercely In the Arena of Ideas—
9781737176343 Hardcover/
9781737176350 eBook

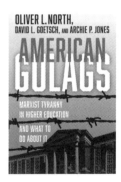

American Gulags: Marxist Tyranny in Higher Education and What to Do About It—
9781956454062 Hardcover/
9781956454079 eBook